THE CRIMES OF JACK THE RIPPER

THE CRIMES OF JACK THE RIPPER

Paul Roland

ARCTURUS

Acknowledgements

The author wishes to express his gratitude to the following for providing access to a wealth of original archive material and impeccably researched articles: *Ripper Notes: The International Journal For Ripper Studies* (Inklings Press) and www.casebook.org, the unrivalled on-line resource for Ripper studies. Also to the following for their invaluable and exhaustive books on the subject: Stewart Evans and Paul Gainey, *The Lodger – The Arrest And Escape Of Jack the Ripper* (Century) and Philip Sugden, *The Complete History Of Jack the Ripper* (Robinson). Finally the author wishes to thank Paul Begg, Executive Editor of *Ripperologist* magazine, for casting his expert eye over the manuscript at the eleventh hour and for his invaluable suggestions.

ARCTURUS

This edition published in 2010 by Arcturus Publishing Limited
26/27 Bickels Yard, 151–153 Bermondsey Street,
London SE1 3HA

ISBN: 978-1-84837-648-9
AD000133EN

Printed in China

CONTENTS

THE MYTH OF JACK THE RIPPER

 On the gloomy afternoon of Tuesday, 2 October 1888, carpenter Frederick Wildborn entered a dank, dark cellar in the new Metropolitan Police headquarters which was then under construction on the Thames Embankment and discovered a large brown paper parcel tied with string. When it was opened it was found to contain the dismembered, decomposing torso of an unidentified female whose severed arm had been fished out of the Thames a few weeks earlier. Her head and the remaining limbs were never recovered. This gruesome discovery was the first in a series of macabre 'torso murders' which were to haunt the recently formed Criminal Investigation Department (CID) over the next 12 months.

At first the police suspected they might be the work of Jack the Ripper, the Whitechapel murderer, who had apparently and inexplicably gone to ground after committing a number of brutal murders earlier that autumn, but the nature of the mutilations suggested otherwise. Evidently there was more than one psychopath stalking the streets of London, despatching his victims with impunity under the very noses of Scotland Yard.

Incredibly, neither the Ripper nor the torso murderer were ever identified, arrested or charged. But while the latter remains a footnote in the history of crime, his evil twin continues to exert a macabre fascination more than a century later. And it's all in the name – a sobriquet created by an unscrupulous but enterprising journalist to keep the killings on the front page and raise the stakes in a cut-throat circulation war. Thanks to this macabre appellation, Jack the Ripper is now lodged in the popular imagination as the personification of the debauched Victorian gentleman, a real-life Mr

Hyde freed from the subconscious of respectable society to embody its repressed sexuality. And yet, the reality was very different. The evidence presented in the following pages clearly contradicts the popular image of the top-hatted and cloaked aristocrat cutting through the swirling London fog with a small black bag, hell bent on ridding the streets of sin.

Hoaxes and wild theories

Unfortunately, any effort to identify the Ripper is made more difficult by the fog of confusion generated by those keen to advance their spurious speculations and fanciful conspiracy theories involving secret societies, eminent surgeons, Satanists and even members of the royal family – occasionally all four – whom we are asked to believe happily came together in a convoluted conspiracy to save England and the Establishment.

Some of the theories that have been put forward are more plausible than others, but nothing pertaining to the Whitechapel murders can be taken at face value. In addition to the 'Dear Boss' letters, which gave birth to the name Jack the Ripper and which are now considered to have been a hoax, there have been more recent attempts to promote seemingly forged documents as genuine artefacts of the period, the notorious Maybrick 'Ripper Diary' being a case in point. More recently an aggressive publicity campaign by crime writer Patricia Cornwell to prove the case against her favoured suspect, the painter Walter Sickert, has only served to add more misinformation to the mix.

In contrast, this book has arisen from a thorough and impartial investigation focusing on a re-examination of the facts as contained in the official Scotland Yard files, the original post-mortem reports and contemporary witness statements as well as the private correspondence of detectives and police officials who had been assigned to, or had overseen, the case. I have aimed to strip away decades of myth and misconception to reveal which, if any, of the usual suspects has a case to answer, while remaining aware that the murders may not have been the work of a single individual.

If these crimes were being investigated today, what would the authorities consider to be the vital clues? How would their profilers describe England's first serial killer and which of the usual suspects would they be looking to convict?

Paul Roland, June 2006

CHAPTER **1** | THE RIPPER'S WORLD

In 1887 Queen Victoria celebrated her Golden Jubilee with much pomp and pageantry. Since her accession, the British Empire had swallowed up colonies as far apart as Canada and the Caribbean, India and Australia, Africa and Asia and was now so extensive that it was said the sun never set upon it.

Britannia not only ruled the waves, but through the notable Christian virtues of self-discipline, enterprise and 'honourable' conquest she also possessed one quarter of the surface of the earth, its people and their wealth. The dour, white-haired mother of the nation now presided over the largest and most prosperous empire the world had ever seen. Britain's industrialists had capitalized on the Empire's formidable resources in both manpower and material, so that by 1870 the United Kingdom could boast

foreign trade figures four times greater than those of the United States.

Industrial marvels

London, the jewel in this imperial crown, had been linked to all of Britain's major cities by a rapidly expanding rail network in a formidable undertaking to rival that of the building of the Egyptian pyramids. Passengers could now travel to and from the metropolis in comfort on journeys that took hours instead of days and traders could transport both raw materials and finished goods to a reliable timetable, making the erratic stagecoach and canal system almost redundant at a stroke. The project had been overseen by the great architect of Victorian regeneration, Isambard Kingdom Brunel. But though Brunel had the vision, the laborious task was realized by a largely

Mother of the nation: Queen Victoria, seen here with the grieving family of Princess Alice, ruled Britain from 1837 to 1901

immigrant workforce who cut through the countryside with pick and shovel to lay 25,000 km (15,530 miles) of track, each length of rail having to be manhandled into position and every spike driven in by hand. Not even nature was permitted to impede the progress of this grand imperial project. Hills were dynamited, forests were flattened and the river Avon was spanned by Brunel's iron suspension bridge which was duly declared a marvel of 19th-century engineering.

Productivity had not slackened since the Queen had opened the Great Exhibition in the vast glass-covered People's Palace (later Crystal Palace) in 1851 to display the best of British ingenuity and enterprise. British goods and raw materials were being exported around the world in British-built ships, earning the country the title 'the workshop of the world', although many unscrupulous employers seized on this appellation as an entitlement to exploit their underpaid female workers and to ignore child labour laws.

Family expectations

Victoria, who had nine children and 37 great-grandchildren, was fiercely proud of her image as the widowed mother of the nation and she expected Britain's middle- and upper-class daughters to be as dutiful and unselfish as she had been. They were to be unquestioningly obedient to their fathers while they lived at home and subservient to their husbands after their marriage. Denied the vote and equal rights, they were also to forgo any intellectual aspirations and instead devote themselves to their husbands' happiness. As for their physical needs, they were expected to repress their own sexuality, which meant squeezing themselves into tortuously tight corsets and shapeless dresses which coyly covered every inch of flesh, rendering them as sexless as a tea cosy. Some inhibited individuals went so far as to cover the legs of their pianos to avoid embarrassment.

The pressures of maintaining a prim and proper façade meant that displays of emotion were frowned upon. Sadness was safely channelled into the cloying sentimentality of popular songs, 'difficult' spiritual questions were given glib reassurances by orthodox religion and grief was acknowledged by the ritual practices of mourning. Death became a morbid preoccupation for many people and sex was stifled with taboos. Wives were instructed to 'lie back and think of England' when their husbands demanded their conjugal rights. In respectable society it was considered wrong for a woman to enjoy sex and those who sought their own pleasure were considered shameless and sinful. They were judged as being no better than the harlots who walked the streets of Whitechapel and were condemned from the pulpits as whores of Babylon.

An unequal society

Though women were labelled the 'weaker sex' they were expected to behave with delicacy and decorum, suffering in silence if need be in order to repress their natural instincts, whereas men were allowed a certain latitude as it was thought that they were less able to control 'the passions'. For this reason prostitution was reluctantly tolerated, despite the fact that by the 1880s the problem was endemic, with an estimated 80,000-plus women plying their trade on the streets of the capital.

Women of the lower classes could redeem themselves by going into domestic service or into gainful employment in the factories and sweatshops. Those who were unable, or unwilling, to do so had only themselves to blame if they met a violent end. These 'fallen' or 'unfortunate' women, as they were euphemistically called, served a social need, relieving respectable women of their marital duties. But they were an underclass, thought no more deserving of society's consideration than India's 'untouchables'.

The repression of emotions and the denial of natural desires inevitably led to a proliferation of brothels in side streets across the capital and a marked increase in domestic violence. In the autumn of 1888 the symptoms of this

*The squalid reality
of life for the
underprivileged*

social disease could no longer be contained and erupted in a frenzied orgy of bloodlust. Ironically, it appears that the man responsible for this terrible catharsis may not in fact have been an Englishman.

The high cost of living in Victorian England

In Victoria's England there were 12 pennies (d) to the shilling and 20 shillings (s) to the pound (£). An inexperienced factory girl could expect to be paid as little as 4s a week, piece workers who did menial skilled tasks at home might be lucky to clear 16s a week, while a skilled labourer would consider himself very fortunate if he took home £3 a week. Reasonable lodgings in a poor working-class neighbourhood could be secured for less than 5s a week, but the most common choice of accommodation in the East End was a bed in a hostel for as little as 4d provided you were prepared

to share the room with up to 60 other people. Eight pence would buy more peace and privacy and less chance of being robbed in your sleep.

A family breakfast cooked at home would set you back 1s 4d, a pint of milk being 2d, six eggs for 6d and a pound of bacon for 8d. Other necessities included a box of candles (6d), a newspaper (a halfpenny upwards), a pint of beer (2d) and a packet of cheap cigarettes (2d). The average bus or tram ride within London cost 6d and 2d would buy a ticket to the music hall.

Sweated labour

Period dramas, films and novels tend to romanticize 19th-century London as a quaint backdrop of gas-lit streets, swirling fog and lurid local colour, but the fog was not atmospheric; it was an irritant and contributed significantly to the increase in respiratory ailments which claimed more lives in the latter half of the 19th century than any other illness. And there was certainly nothing romantic about the deplorable conditions in which the inhabitants of the East End were forced to live.

Of the 900,000 inhabitants of the East End, more than 76,000 were concentrated in Whitechapel. Almost half of these were officially classed as living in poverty. Many thousands more eked out a meagre living in factories and sweatshops for 10–18 hours a day in arduous and dangerous conditions for exploitative employers who fined their workforce for every infraction of their draconian regulations. The 1,400 female workers employed by match manufacturers Bryant & May in Bow, for example, were fined half a day's pay for being late and 3d for having dirty feet or an untidy workbench. As they very seldom earned more than 4s a week, they could be left with little to

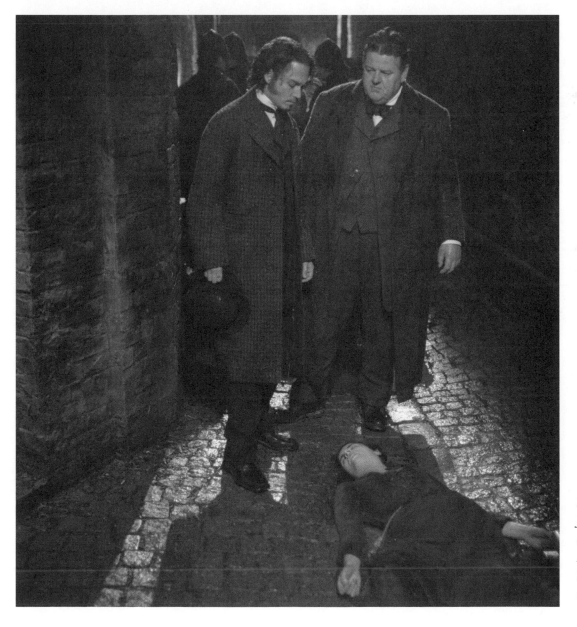

Ripper revisited: Johnny Depp as a psychic Inspector Abberline and Robbie Coltrane in the film From Hell

Beware 'phossy jaw': in addition to poor pay and long hours, life held hidden dangers for the match girls of London

live on if they were unfortunate enough to work under a foreman who took a dislike to their appearance or their demeanour.

Privation and exploitation

In addition to the poor pay and long hours the match girls risked a debilitating condition known as 'phossy jaw', brought on by the constant inhalation of noxious phosphorous fumes. Those who succumbed were summarily dismissed. It was only after their case had been highlighted by social reformer Annie Besant in an article entitled 'White Slavery In London' that a public outcry forced the employers to offer certain concessions. But even after the implementation of the reforms (including the formation of a union), life remained harsh for the match girls and their fellow factory workers. Under such circumstances many were tempted to take their chances on the street. Anything was better than admitting themselves into the care of the public workhouse, which was not much better than a prison.

Piece workers suffered privation and exploitation to a similar degree, although they had the advantage of working from home which meant that they could enlist members of their family to increase their productivity and thereby their earnings. For this reason many children were denied a basic education, even though attendance had been made compulsory by the 1870 Education Act. Garment workers could earn as much as one shilling a day; a shirt finisher, for example, was paid 3d per dozen shirts for which she would have to sew on the linings, make the buttonholes and sew on the buttons. But home workers were often no better off than sweated labour. Fur pickers, for example, risked respiratory disorders from breathing in the fine fibres which they were surrounded by night and day.

A London fog

'As the east wind brings up the exhalations of the Essex and Kentish marshes, and as the damp-laden winter air prevents the dispersion of the partly consumed carbon from hundreds of thousands of chimneys, the strangest atmospheric compound known to science fills the valley of the Thames . . . Not only does a strange and worse than Cimmerian darkness hide familiar landmarks from the sights, but the taste and sense of smell are offended by the unhallowed compound of flavours, and all things become greasy and clammy to the touch . . . It is almost unnecessary to add that the dangers of the streets, great at all times, are immeasurably increased in foggy weather; and that the advantages of being able to dive into that unnatural darkness after a successful robbery are thoroughly appreciated by the predatory classes.'

(*Dickens' Dictionary Of London*
by Charles Dickens, 1883)

Sin or starve

'I don't suppose I'll live much longer and that's another thing that pleases me.'

(Anonymous Whitechapel prostitute)

In Victorian England even the prostitutes were divided by class. In the West End the more audacious streetwalkers strolled proudly among the theatre and concert hall crowds wearing red bandanas and carrying a short cane. The youngest and most attractive could demand several pounds from their wealthy clients and lived in comparative comfort.

But the East End was another world. There business was conducted down dark alleyways, in the shelter of a doorway and in backyards which were always open to the street. Nobody bothered to lock their front doors for the simple reason they had nothing worth stealing. If the customer wanted privacy there were common lodging houses and brothels on almost every corner which offered a maze of filthy boxrooms for hire by the hour. The bedding was rarely changed, but the clients didn't complain. They were not inclined to wash themselves either.

Contemporary social commentator John Binny sketched a vibrant picture of the wretched women he observed during his explorations of the East End: 'They live in the greatest poverty, covered with rags and filth, and many

'The East End was another world ... business was conducted down dark alleyways'

of them covered with horrid sores, and eruptions on their body, arms and legs, presenting in many cases a revolting appearance. Many of them have not the delicacy of females and live as pigs in a sty . . . In the middle of the day they sometimes wash their skirt, the only decent garment many of them have – their underclothing being a tissue of rags.'

Frequently prostitution was a means to a more reprehensible end. It was not unknown for a woman to team up with a ruffian who would rob the customer while he was unable to defend himself, beating him senseless so that he couldn't identify his attacker.

A squalid scene

To police the labyrinth of dark alleys, passageways, backyards, courts and closes in the square mile where the murders by Jack the Ripper would take place would have required a force far in excess of the number of officers the Met and City Police could have assembled. Besides, prostitution was not illegal in England at that time, although self-styled 'purity' groups were actively campaigning to drive the sex trade off the streets. They had succeeded in shaming Parliament into raising the age of consent from 13 to 16, and in the summer of 1887 Sir Charles Warren had been pressured into ordering the closure of 200 brothels in

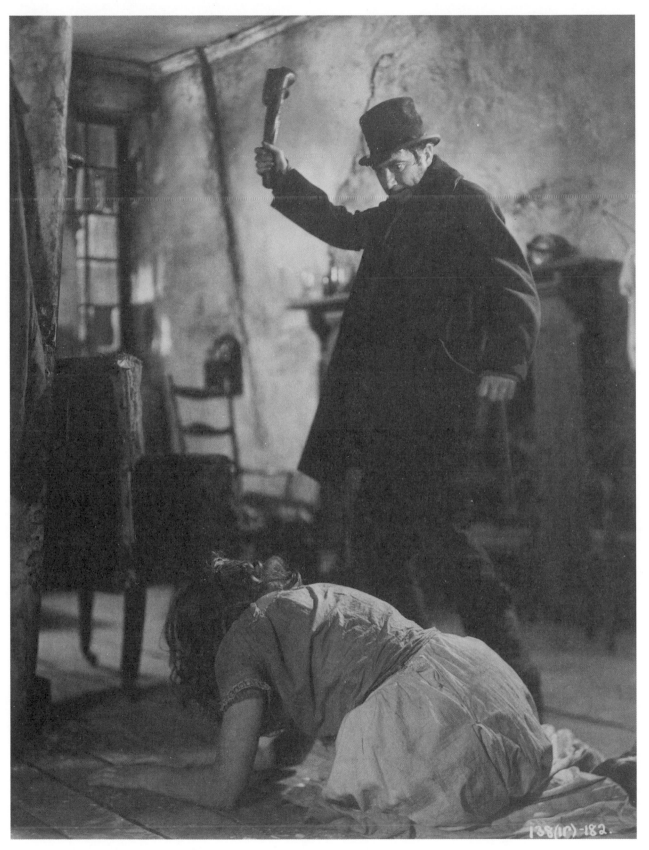

The age of reform: Charles Dickens took on the subject of social oppression in Oliver Twist, *first published in 1837–8*

the East End to appease the reformers who considered them a stain on the conscience of a Christian nation.

But even the most naive reformer must have conceded that the sheer scale of the problem was beyond the powers of the police to control, or even to contain. Whitechapel alone had 63 brothels and boasted in excess of 1,200 prostitutes.

Many older women resorted to selling themselves for as little as 4d to pay for a night's lodgings. The most desperate settled for 2d, the price of sharing a crowded room slumped over a rope in a doss house. It was only marginally more comfortable than sleeping in the street. Binny described such wretches as being 'bloated, dissipated, and brutal in appearance; others pale and wasted by want and suffering . . . they often indulge in the grossest indecencies . . . with old grey-headed men on the very edge of the grave. Many of these women are old convicted thieves of sixty years of age upwards. Strange to say, old men and boys go with these withered crones, and sometimes fashionable gentlemen on a lark are to be seen walking arm in arm with them, and even to enter their houses.'

The patronage of these 'fashionable gentlemen' led some of the younger women to hope that they might one day be rescued from the streets by a wealthy man. But too often their fate was to die of consumption, starvation or drink. For a few, fate had something far worse in store.

The East End

'It was the best of times, it was the worst of times.' (Charles Dickens, A Tale of Two Cities)

On the afternoon of 6 August 1888, just hours before the first Whitechapel murder, the Bank Holiday crowd at Alexandra Palace were treated to a number of diverting entertainments, one of which involved a certain Professor Baldwin parachuting from a hot air balloon suspended 305m (1,000ft) above the crowd.

Had the fearless professor instead offered flights over the capital to anyone brave enough to climb into the basket, their delight would surely have turned to disbelief as the balloon drifted over the squalid streets of the East End. With its warren of narrow, shabby alleyways, smoke-blackened tenements, derelict warehouses and gutters awash with raw effluent, Whitechapel, Spitalfields and Aldgate looked as if they had been gouged out of the dark heart of Calcutta and deposited just a stone's throw from the centre of the Empire in a gesture of defiance. This festering sore of criminality and vice was not merely

'Too often their fate was to die of consumption, starvation or drink'

considered an affront to genteel sensibilities; the pillars of polite society argued it was also threatening to infect the more affluent parts of the city and disrupt the social order of the Empire from within.

Even on that mild, wet August Bank Holiday afternoon, Whitechapel and its environs appeared dusted with fuller's earth. The long, featureless rows of terraced housing, their windows blind with grime, were uniformly grey with only the dull red bricks, open doorways and faded curtains to distinguish each grim dwelling from its neighbour. On the main thoroughfare horse-drawn wagons clattered over cobbles, passing a rude assortment of shops, many bearing the name of their foreign proprietors who had fled persecution in Russia and eastern Europe. And on almost every corner a public house offered a respite from reality behind the frosted glass with the promise of a sentimental song interrupted by a brawl in the public bar which might spill out onto the street.

Coaching: a more picturesque image of Victorian times

A family of acrobats, 1890. Stiltwalkers, hurdygurdymen and jugglers were among other street performers of the time

Off the main thoroughfare the air was thick with the acrid stench of rotting fruit, fresh fish and roasting chestnuts. The inhabitants were accustomed to the noise of hawkers' cries competing with barrel organs, street performers, soapbox preachers and a wide selection of drunkards yelling abuse at the world in general. Everywhere the East End was heaving with humanity and reeking of dilapidation and decay.

A cruel place

Contrary to such pictures of the East End painted by Dickens and his contemporaries, Victorian England was a far less violent place in the years between 1870 and the outbreak of the First World War than in the previous half-century. In fact, reported incidents of murder were approximately half what they had been in the previous period. But random cruelty was a feature of daily life south and east of the River Thames. There is some truth in the accusation made by certain contemporary writers that the inhabitants of Whitechapel were inured to brutality from an early age. Slaughterhouses were open to the streets and children would dare one another to sneak in to see the animals having their throats slit.

It was said that inhabitants were so familiar with the sounds of drunken brawls and domestic disputes that they had become deaf to cries for help and immune to the suffering of their fellow citizens. As George Sims, author of *Horrible London*, remarked, 'The spirit of murder hovers over this spot . . . Down from one dark court rings a cry of murder, and a woman, her face hideously gashed, makes across the narrow road, pursued by a howling madman. It is only a drunken husband having a row with his wife.'

But before the end of the year even the most world-weary resident would be sickened by the horrors which spilt onto the streets of Whitechapel.

A tour of Whitechapel

'A horrible black labyrinth, think many people, reeking from end to end with the vilest exhalations; its streets, mere kennels of horrid putrefaction; its every wall, its every object, slimy with the indigenous ooze of the place; swarming with human vermin, whose trade is robbery, and whose recreation is murder; the catacombs of London darker, more tortuous, and more dangerous than those of Rome, and supersaturated with foul life. Others imagine Whitechapel in a pitiful aspect. Outcast London. Black and nasty still, a wilderness of crazy dens into which pallid wastrels crawl to die; where several families lie in each fetid room, and fathers, mothers, and children watch each other starve; where bony, blear-eyed wretches, with everything beautiful, brave, and worthy crushed out of them, and nothing of the glory and nobleness and jollity of this world within the range of their crippled senses, rasp away their puny lives in the*

A Salvation Army shelter for women in Whitechapel during the late-Victorian era, complete with its ominous message for inmates

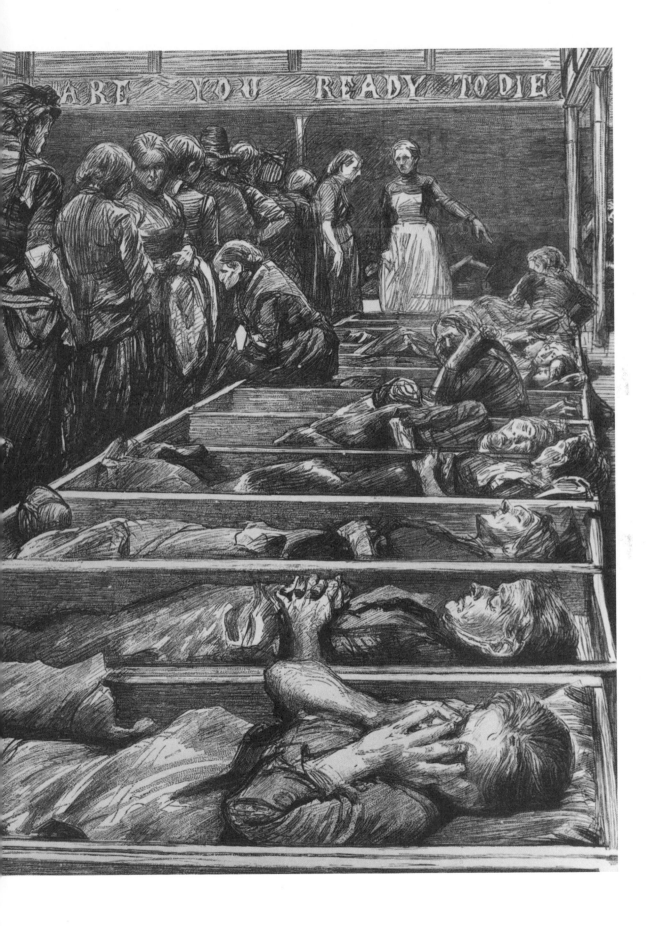

sty of the sweater. Such spots as these there certainly are in Whitechapel, and in other places, but generalities are rarely true, and when applied to a district of London so large as that comprised under the name of Whitechapel, never. For Whitechapel, as understood colloquially, goes some distance beyond the bounds set by the parish authorities of St Mary, and includes much of Aldgate and Spitalfields, besides a not inconsiderable fragment of Mile End.

We make a small excursion into Mansell Street, which is quiet. All about here, and in Great Ailie Street, Tenter Street, and their vicinities, the houses are old, large, of the very shabbiest-genteel aspect, and with a great appearance of being snobbishly ashamed of the odd trades to which many of their rooms are devoted. Shirt-making in buried basements, packing-case, or, perhaps, cardboard box-making, on the ground-floor; and glimpses of very dirty bald heads, bending over cobbling, or the sorting of "old clo'," through the cracked and rag-stuffed upper windows. Jewish names – Isaacs, Levy, Israel, Jacobs, Rubinsky, Moses, Aaron – wherever names appear, and frequent inscriptions in the homologous letters of Hebrew. Many of these inscriptions are on the windows of eating-houses, whose interior mysteries are hidden by muslin curtains; and we occasionally find a shop full of Hebrew books, and showing in its window remarkable little nick-nacks appertaining to synagogue worship, amid plaited tapers of various colours.

Petticoat Lane is before us . . . As Hog Lane, with its sunny hedgerows and one or two pleasant citizens' houses; as Petticoat Lane, with its thievery and squalor and old clothes; and as Middlesex Street, with its warehouses, this thoroughfare has lived through a chequered existence . . .

At the end we have Artillery Lane, Gun Street, and Raven Row. Dirt, rag shops and small beer-houses. Sometimes a peep down a clogged grating, or over a permanent shutter, into the contaminated breath of a sweater's lair, where poisoned human lives are spun into the apparel which clothes the bodies of wholesome men. Through White's Row, or Dorset Street, with its hideous associations, into busy Commercial Street, with its traffic, its warehouses, its early lights, and the bright spot in this unpleasant neighbourhood, Toynbee Hall and Institute, and St Jude's Church, whose beautiful wall-mosaic of Time, Death, and Judgement has its own significance here, in the centre of the scattered spots which are the recent sites of satanic horrors.

Fashion Street, Flower and Dean Street, Thrawl Street, Wentworth Street. Through which shall we go to Brick Lane? Black and noisome, the road sticky with slime, and palsied houses, rotten from chimney to cellar, leaning together, apparently by the mere coherence of their ingrained corruption. Dark, silent, uneasy shadows passing and crossing – human vermin in this reeking sink, like goblin *exhalations from all that is noxious around. Women with sunken, black-rimmed eyes, whose pallid faces appear and vanish by the light of an occasional gas-lamp, and look so like ill-covered skulls that we start at their stare. Horrible London? Yes.*

Some years ago, it was fashionable to "slum" – to walk gingerly about in dirty streets, with great heroism, and go back West again, with a firm conviction that "something must be done". And something must. Children must not be left in these unscoured corners. Their fathers and mothers are hopeless, and

must not be allowed to rear a numerous and equally hopeless race. Light the streets better, certainly; but what use in building better houses for these poor creatures to render as foul as those that stand? The inmates may ruin the character of a house, but no house can alter the character of its inmates.'

Extract from *The Palace Journal* by Arthur G. Morrison (24 April, 1889), which vividly illustrates the terrible poverty and squalor of life in Whitechapel towards the end of the 19th century.

A street market with gas lighting in east London

CHAPTER **2** | THE MURDER CASEBOOK

In defiance of the overcast skies, many middle-class Londoners made the most of August Bank Holiday Monday, 1888, by taking day trips to the south coast or excursions into the countryside. Those who chose to remain in the capital were spoilt for choice as to how to pass the day. Almost all the customary attractions were within a short omnibus ride of the West End and were still a novelty. For half a crown a family of four could spend an agreeable afternoon gaping at the animals in the Zoological Gardens in Regent's Park, marvelling at the lifelike figures at Madame Tussaud's or taking in a tour at the Tower of London and still have change for refreshments and the ride home. A couple of shillings would cover entrance to the exotic orchid houses at Crystal Palace or the manicured gardens at Kew, while edification and culture could be had for free at the Natural History Museum and Science Museum in fashionable Kensington or at the National Portrait Gallery, which relocated from South Kensington to Bethnal Green in 1885. The advantage of museums was that they offered both diversion and shelter should the skies open unexpectedly.

In contrast, many of those living south of the river enjoyed the day in a more modest manner. Martha Tabram (aka Martha Turner) and her friend Pearly Poll spent the day cadging drinks in various public houses around Whitechapel. Martha, who for some reason had told her new friend that her name was 'Emma', was a plump, 39-year-old married mother of two teenage sons, with a swarthy complexion. She had been separated from her husband Henry, a foreman furniture packer, for nine years and had been living with William Turner, a carpenter, in George Street, Whitechapel, supplementing their income by hawking trinkets for a halfpenny an item. But her fondness for ale, and anything stronger when she could afford it, had led her to rely on prostitution. Turner had given up on her and Martha was in need of a few coppers for a room. Poll's offer to team up for the night must have seemed like a practical solution.

By 10pm they had befriended two soldiers at the Angel and Crown, who said they were stationed at the Tower of London, and were confident of procuring enough change to pay for their lodgings. Shortly before midnight the pair separated. Polly led her client into nearby Angel Alley and Martha staggered arm in arm with her customer round the corner to George Yard, off Whitechapel High Street. Half an hour later Polly and her punter bid each other goodnight and she wandered off giving no further thought to her friend.

A body discovered

It was not until 4.45am the next morning that John Reaves, a tenant at 37 George Yard Buildings, came upon the lifeless body of a woman sprawled on the first-floor landing as he made his way to work. It was Martha Tabram. She was lying on her back with her legs apart and her long black jacket, dark green skirt and brown petticoat pushed up to the waist, suggesting that she had

been killed while engaged in intercourse. Her fists were clenched in her death agony and thick sticky blood pooled around her on the flagstones from her black bonnet to her side-spring boots. Reaves stepped over the body and legged it down the stairs and out into the street in search of a policeman.

Under the headline 'The Murder in Whitechapel', the following extract from *The Times*, dated 10 August 1888, details what Dr Killeen, a local physician, discovered when he was called to the scene that morning. The fact that the murder went unreported for three days suggests that both the press and the police were slow to realize the significance of the Martha Tabram murder.

'Dr T R Killeen, of 68, Brick-lane, said that he was called to the deceased, and found her dead. She had 39 stabs on the body. She had been dead some three hours. Her age was about 36, and the body was very well nourished. Witness had since made a post mortem examination of the body. The left lung was penetrated in five places, and the right lung was penetrated in two places. The heart, which was rather fatty, was penetrated in one place, and that would be sufficient to cause death. The liver was healthy, but was penetrated in five places, the spleen was penetrated in two places, and the stomach, which was perfectly healthy, was penetrated in six places. The witness did not think all the*

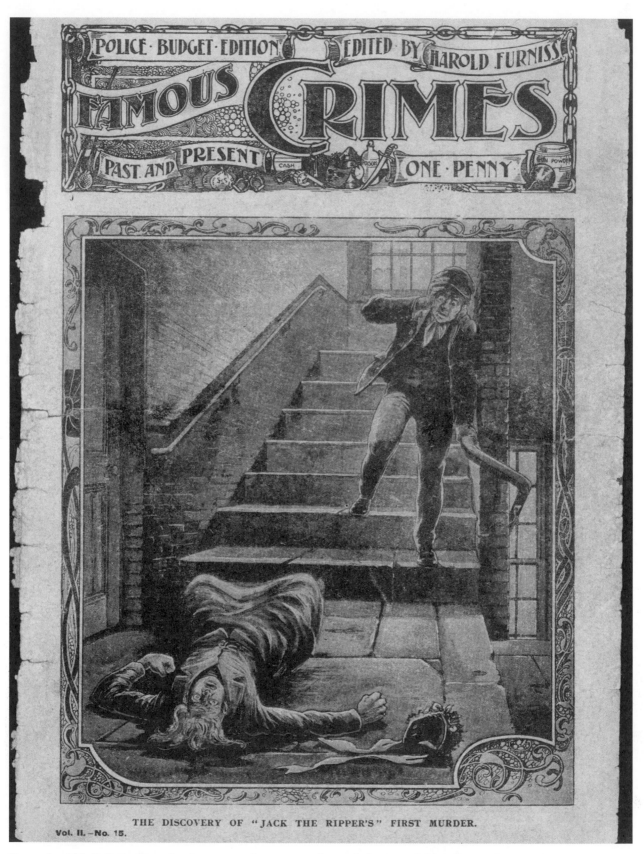

POLICE · BUDGET · EDITION   EDITED · BY · HAROLD · FURNISS

FAMOUS CRIMES

PAST · AND · PRESENT   ONE · PENNY

THE DISCOVERY OF "JACK THE RIPPER'S" FIRST MURDER.

Vol. II.—No. 15.

Penny dreadful: Jack the Ripper's crimes were often portrayed in melodramatic fashion for popular consumption

wounds were inflicted with the same instrument. The wounds generally might have been inflicted with a knife, but such an instrument could not have inflicted one of the wounds, which went through the chestbone. His opinion was that one of the wounds was inflicted by some kind of dagger, and that all of them had been caused during life. The Coroner [remarked that]...it was one of the most dreadful murders any one could imagine. The man must have been a perfect savage to inflict such a number of wounds on a defenceless woman in such a way.'

It was established that Martha had been murdered between 1.50 and 3.30am. At the coroner's inquest, resident Elizabeth Mahonney had testified that she had returned at 1.50 to her rooms at 47 George Yard and seen no one on the landing. An hour and 40 minutes later cab driver Alfred Crow ascended the wide stone staircase to his rooms at number 35 and noticed a woman lying on the landing, but thought little of it as vagrants were in the habit of sleeping off their drink at George Yard. None of the residents had heard a sound during the night, although Mrs Hewitt, the building superintendent's wife, had heard a cry of 'murder' earlier that evening, but hadn't informed her husband as it appeared to originate from outside and such disturbances were an almost nightly occurrence in the area.

The reason no one heard the poor woman's cry for help was addressed by the *Illustrated Police News*, a sensationalist tabloid which, despite the title, had no association with the authorities. It speculated that her cries had been stifled. She had been 'throttled while being held down and the face and head being so swollen and distorted in consequence that her real features are not discernible'.

The *Daily News* added that Dr Killeen had concluded that there may have been two assailants, one evidently left-handed and the other right-handed and that the wounds had been inflicted by two weapons, one a penknife and the other either a dagger or bayonet.

A soldier under suspicion

Suspicion immediately fell on the soldier who appeared to have been the last person to have seen Martha alive. PC Barrett, the officer who had been called to the scene by Reaves, had seen a soldier loitering in George Yard at 2am, at the time the murder might have occurred. It is very likely that this was the same soldier Martha had been keeping company with two hours earlier when she parted with Pearly Poll. When PC Barrett approached him and asked what he was doing at this hour the soldier replied that he was waiting for a friend who had gone with a woman.

PC Barrett described the soldier as a private in the Grenadier Guards who had a good conduct badge pinned to his tunic but no medals. He was in his early to mid-twenties, of average height (about 175cm/5ft 9in) with a fair complexion, dark hair and a small brown moustache turned up at the ends. But when an identification parade was arranged at the Tower on the morning of 8 August, the constable picked out two men who verified each other's story and were allowed to return to the ranks. That may have been Scotland Yard's first fatal mistake. The soldiers were almost certainly the killers and, had they been questioned more thoroughly, Martha Tabram might not be acknowledged today as the Ripper's first victim.

The body in Bucks Row

Fate was particularly cruel to Mary Ann 'Polly' Nichols. She should have been safe in bed on the morning of 31 August 1888 but was instead found sprawled in the street gutted like one of the pigs in nearby Spitalfields market. She had earned her bed and board three times that day but had drunk it all away. Had she saved just a few coppers, she would not have been soliciting for her final customer of the evening when she fell foul of Jack the Ripper.

Polly Nichols was a short, stout, middle-aged, married woman with five children who had been separated from her family because of her fondness for alcohol and was forced to rely on the charitable ministrations of Lambeth Workhouse. But shortly before her death she had tried to get back on the straight and narrow by taking a position as a domestic servant to a respectable couple in Wandsworth. Her new-found employment enabled her to leave the workhouse and find lodgings at Thrawl Street with an elderly room-mate who described her as clean, quiet and inoffensive, so long as she was sober. Her new employers evidently found her agreeable too and something of her state of mind at the time can be gleaned from her final letter to her estranged husband, which paints a very different picture of a penniless streetwalker to the blowsy, foul-mouthed bawd of popular fiction.

'I just write to say that you will be glad to know that I am settled in my new place and going on all right up to now. My people went out yesterday, and have not returned, so I am left in charge. All has been newly done up. They are teetotallers and religious, so I ought to get on. They are very nice people, and I have not too much to do. I hope you are alright and the boy has work. So good-bye for the present. –
From yours truly POLLY
Answer soon, please, and let me know how you are.'

A fatal error

However, the demon drink bedevilled Polly and during a moment of weakness she gave in to temptation, stealing a bundle of clothes from her employers for which she was summarily dismissed. On the night of her death she was turned away from her old lodgings in Thrawl Street

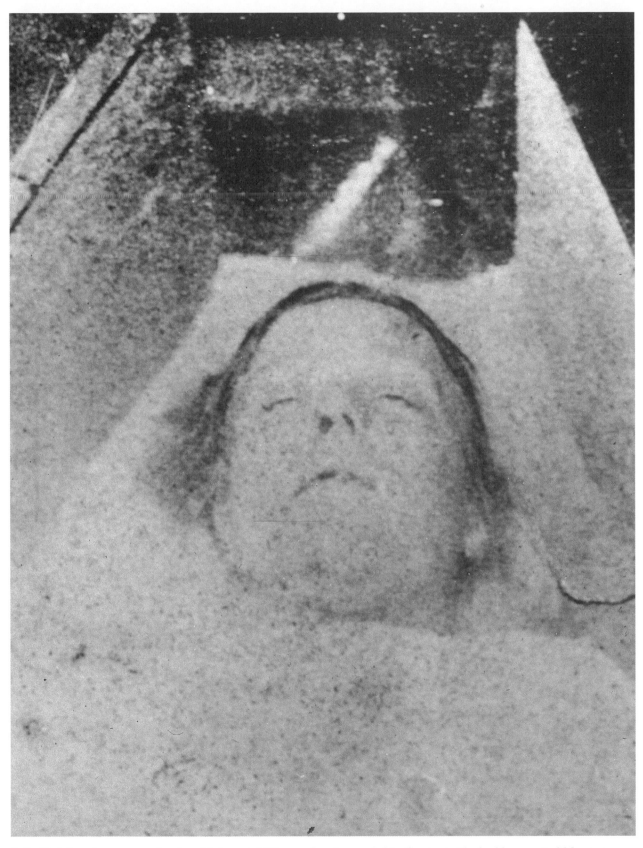

Polly Nichols, who was murdered on 31 August 1888, was found sprawled in the street. She had been gutted like a pig

because she didn't have the 4d for the room. Undaunted, she told them to hold her bed for her and that she would be back shortly with the money.

'I'll soon get my doss money,' she laughed as she staggered down the street. 'See what a jolly bonnet I've got now!'

Polly was proud of her new black straw bonnet with the black trim. Beneath it her brown hair was turning prematurely grey, framing her sallow skin and brown eyes. She wore a rustic brown, double-breasted overcoat, a new frock of the same colour, a white chest flannel, black stockings and side-spring boots with steel-tipped heels to save wear and tear.

At the corner of Whitechapel Road and Osborn Street she chanced to meet her former room-mate, Ellen Holland, who vainly tried to persuade Polly to come back with her. 'I've had my lodging money three times today and I've spent it,' Polly boasted. 'It won't be long before I'll be back.' It was 2.30am when they parted. Ellen was the last person to see Polly alive.

Just over an hour later two workmen walking down the narrow north end of Bucks Row towards the Board School where the street widens came upon what they assumed to be a tarpaulin discarded on the pavement by the entrance to Brown's Stable Yard. In the early-morning gloom, with only a feeble street lamp across the way, they couldn't make out what it was until they stood over it. It was the body of a woman lying on her back with her skirts up around her waist. They adjusted them to afford her some dignity before summoning a policeman, PC Mizen. 'She looks to me to be either dead or drunk,' said one, urging the constable to investigate. 'But for my part I think she is dead.' Meanwhile, another policeman, PC Neil, stumbled upon the body and was shortly joined by the two workmen and PC Mizen.

She was indeed dead, although no one realized the extent of her mutilations until she had been removed to the mortuary for closer examination. In the early-morning light all the police knew was that her throat had been cut so violently that her head had been almost severed from her body. Her eyes were wide open, gazing up at the blood-red sky. When the horse-drawn ambulance came to take her away her new black bonnet was tossed into the cart beside her.

The Whitechapel murders

The following extract from *The Times*, 3 September 1888, is of special interest as it is the first indication that the police were considering that the murders might be the work of a serial killer. It also highlights the question of how the Ripper managed to elude a strong police presence in the area.

'Up to a late hour last evening the police had obtained no clue to the perpetrator of the latest of the three murders which

have so recently taken place in Whitechapel, and there is, it must be acknowledged, after their exhaustive investigation of the facts, no ground for blaming the officers in charge should they fail in unravelling the mystery surrounding the crime. The murder, in the early hours of Friday morning last, of the woman now known as Mary Ann Nichols, has so many points of similarity with the murder of two other women in the same neighbourhood – one Martha Tabram, as recently as August 7, and the other less than 12 months previously – that the police admit their belief that the three crimes are the work of one individual. All three women were of the class called "unfortunates," each so very poor, that robbery could have formed no motive for the crime, and each was murdered in such a similar fashion, that doubt as to the crime being the work of one and the same villain almost vanishes, particularly when it is remembered that all three murders were committed within a distance of 300 yards from each other.

These facts have led the police to almost abandon the idea of a gang being abroad to wreak vengeance on women of this class for not supplying them with money. Detective Inspector Abberline, of the Criminal Investigation Department, and Detective Inspector Helson, J Division, are both of opinion that only one person, and that a man, had a hand in the latest murder. It is understood that the investigation into the George-yard mystery is proceeding hand-in-hand

with that of Bucks Row. It is considered unlikely that the woman could have entered a house, been murdered, and removed to Bucks Row within a period of one hour and a quarter. The woman who last saw her alive, and whose name is Nelly Holland, was a fellow-lodger with the deceased in Thrawl Street, and is positive as to the time being 2:30. Police constable Neil, 79 J, who found the body, reports the time as 3:45. Bucks Row is a secluded place, from having tenements on one side only. The constable has been severely questioned as to his "working" of his "beat" on that night, and states that he was last on the spot where he found the body not more than half an hour previously – that is to say, at 3:15.

The beat is a very short one, and quickly walked over would not occupy more than 12 minutes. He neither heard a cry nor saw any one. Moreover, there are three watchmen on duty at night close to the spot, and neither one heard a cry to cause alarm. It is not true, says Constable Neil, who is a man of nearly 20 years' service, that he was called to the body by two men. He came upon it as he walked, and flashing his lantern to examine it, he was answered by the lights from two other constables at either end of the street. These officers had seen no man leaving the spot to attract attention, and the mystery is most complete . . .

The deceased was lying lengthways, and her left hand touched the gate. With the aid of his lamp he examined the body and saw blood oozing from a wound in the throat. Deceased was lying upon her back with her clothes disarranged. Witness felt her arm, which was quite warm from the joints upwards, while her eyes were wide open. Her bonnet was off her head and was lying by her right side, close by the left hand. Witness then heard a constable passing Brady Street, and he called to him. Witness said to him, "Run at once for Dr. Llewellyn." Seeing another constable in Baker's Row, witness despatched him for the ambulance . . .

[PC Neil] had not heard any disturbance that night. The farthest he had been that night was up Baker's Row to the Whitechapel Road, and was never far away from the spot. The Whitechapel Road was a busy thoroughfare in the early morning, and he saw a number of women in that road, apparently on their way home. At that time any one could have got away. Witness examined the ground while the doctor was being sent for. In answer to a juryman, the witness said he did not see any trap in the road. He examined the road, but could not see any marks of wheels . . .

Mr. Henry Llewellyn, surgeon, of 152, Whitechapel Road, stated that at 4 o'clock on Friday morning he was called by the last witness to Bucks Row . . . On reaching Bucks Row he found deceased lying flat on her back on the pathway, her legs being extended. Deceased was quite dead, and she had severe injuries to her throat. Her hands and wrists were cold, but the lower extremities were quite warm . . . He should say the deceased had not been dead more than half an hour . . . There was very little blood round the neck, and there were no marks of any struggle, or of blood as though the body had been dragged . . . That morning he made a post mortem examination of the body.

It was that of a female of about 40 or 45 years. Five of the teeth were missing, and there was a slight laceration of the tongue. There was a bruise running along the lower part of the jaw on the right side of the face. That might have been caused by a blow from a fist or pressure from a thumb. There was a circular bruise on the left side of the face, which also might have been inflicted by the pressure of the fingers. On the left side of the neck, about 1in. below the jaw, there was an incision about 4in. in length, and ran from a point immediately below the ear. On the same side, but an inch below, and commencing about 1in. in front of it, was a circular incision, which terminated in a point about 3in. below the right jaw. That incision completely severed all the tissues down to the vertebrae. The large vessels of the neck on both sides were severed. The incision was about 8in. in length. The cuts must have been caused by a long-bladed knife, moderately sharp, and used with great violence.

No blood was found on the breast, either of the body or clothes. There were no injuries about the body until just below the lower part of the abdomen. Two or three inches from the left side was a wound running in a jagged manner.

Bucks Row – now known as Darward Street – east London, where the body of Polly Nichols was found, lying in the gutter

The wound was a very deep one, and the tissues were cut through. There were several incisions running across the abdomen. There were also three or four similar cuts, running downwards, on the right side, all of which had been caused by a knife which had been used violently and downwards. The injuries were from left to right, and might have been done by a left-handed person. All the injuries had been caused by the same instrument.'

Bloodhounds

Shortly before Christmas 1887, Detective Inspector Frederick George Abberline had been honoured with a presentation dinner at the Unicorn Tavern in Shoreditch to commemorate his 25 years' service in the Metropolitan Police, the past 14 of which he had spent in the East End. It was a grand affair with effusive speeches, good food and plenty of locally brewed beer, at the end of which the modest and meticulous West Country career policeman was presented with a gold watch by a grateful citizens' committee and his many colleagues at H Division in recognition of his contribution to keeping a cap on crime in the roughest district in London. Abberline, who was by then 45 years old, was looking forward to taking up his new post at Scotland Yard to which he had been seconded at the request of the top brass at the newly formed Criminal Investigation Division, or CID as it became known. He could not have imagined that within a year he would be called back to Whitechapel to lead the hunt for a multiple murderer who would ultimately elude both himself and the most experienced detectives in the country.

Abberline knew all the shady characters in every back street of the East End and he didn't attain such knowledge sitting behind his desk. But when he returned to his old hunting ground in the autumn of 1888 he was portly and balding, with a soft-spoken manner no self-respecting villain would have found intimidating. Colleague Walter Dew (another member of the Ripper team) thought he looked more like a bank manager or solicitor, but Abberline was a copper of the old school, a human bloodhound who wouldn't give up on a trail once he'd got the scent. If anyone could catch the Whitechapel murderer he could.

A dangerous labyrinth

Abberline was initially optimistic about catching the man responsible for the deaths of Martha Tabram and Polly Nichols. But it soon became clear that the quarry knew the labyrinth of alleyways in even more detail than he did. The scale of the problem can be gleaned from a contemporary account written by American journalist R. Harding Davis, who was taken on a tour of the murder sites by another member of Abberline's team, Inspector Henry Moore.

Moore cut a formidable figure in the East End. He was muscular and evidently able to handle himself, but even so he carried a maple-coloured cane of solid iron in anticipation of trouble, 'for those who don't know me'. He told Davis:

'I might put two regiments of police in this half-mile of district and half of them would be as completely out of sight and hearing of the others as though they were in separate cells of a prison. To give you an idea of it, my men formed a circle around the spot where one of the murders took place, guarding, they thought, every entrance and approach, and within a few minutes they found fifty people inside the lines. They had come in through two passageways which my men could not find. And then, you know, these people never lock their doors, and the murderer has only to lift the latch of the nearest house and walk through it and out the back way . . .

'What makes it so easy for him is that the women lead him of their own free will to the spot where they know interruption is least likely. It is not as if he had to wait for his chance; they make the chance for him. And then they are so miserable and so hopeless, so utterly lost to all that makes a person want to live, that for the sake of four pence, enough to get drunk on, they will go in any man's company, and run the risk that it is not him. I tell many of them to go home, but they say that they have no home, and when I try to frighten them and speak of the danger they run, they'll laugh and say, "Oh, I know what you mean. I ain't afraid of him. It's the Ripper or the bridge for me [meaning suicide]. What's the odds?" and it's true; that's the worst of it.'

It was customary for Scotland Yard to send experienced men to assist the

*The rookeries –
a row of huddled
dwellings under
the railway arch*

local police when their resources were stretched during a serious investigation. So it was not considered a sign of impatience or lack of confidence in local Inspector Edmund Reid and his men when Chief Inspector Moore and his two colleagues, inspectors Abberline and Andrews, arrived at the Commercial Street police station in Whitechapel with a number of assistants in tow, one of them being Detective Walter Dew, who was later to find fame as the man who arrested Dr Crippen. Their arrival was intended to signal that the investigation was to be stepped up a gear and it also served to repair the damage done to morale by the recent resignation of Assistant Commissioner James Monro, who had quarrelled with his superior, Sir Charles Warren. Monro's replacement was to be Dr Robert Anderson, but ill health prevented Anderson from taking up his post before the beginning of October so Moore, Abberline and Andrews were effectively in charge of the manhunt under the supervision of Chief Inspector Donald Swanson back at Scotland Yard.

Of the three Yard men sent down to Commercial Street, the most overlooked is Inspector Walter Andrews, who had been described by Dew as a 'jovial, gentlemanly man'. He was 41 years of age when he was assigned to the Ripper case and, though he is not featured at all in the official records, it is believed that it is because he was on the trail of one particular

individual, a previously unnamed suspect whose file mysteriously went missing from the archives (see page 137).

As Walter Dew was later to note in his memoirs, 'There are still those who look upon the Whitechapel murders as one of the most ignominious police failures of all time. Failure it certainly was, but I have never regarded it other than an honourable failure.'

And he defended the reputations of the three CID detectives sent to assist the local officers. 'I am satisfied that no better or more efficient men could have been chosen. These three men did everything humanly possible to free Whitechapel of its Terror. They failed because they were up against a problem the like of which the world had never known, and I fervently hope, will never know again.'

Horrible murder in Hanbury Street

'Dark Annie' Chapman was a short, heavy-set woman who had lived most of her life on the streets of the East End. Never an attractive woman, by the time she had turned 45 she looked as if life had knocked her about a bit and she had the bruises to prove it. The first of her three children had died, the second had been institutionalized and the third confined in a home for cripples. Her husband had reputedly drunk himself to death and Annie looked set to follow him. By September 1888 she was destitute and down to borrowing a couple of shillings from her brother to pay for a cheap room

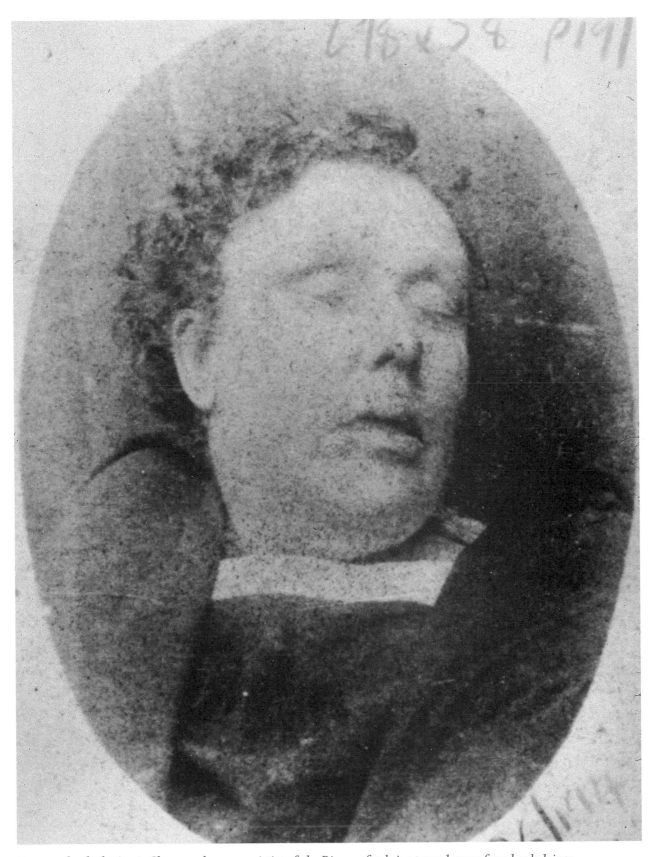

Down on her luck: Annie Chapman became a victim of the Ripper after being turned away from her lodgings

and a meal with the promise to pay him back when she went hop-picking in Kent. But as always, it was just talk. She never left the city.

In the early hours of Saturday 8 September 1888 she was turned away from her lodgings at 35 Dorset Street because she didn't have the necessary 4d for a bed and tottered down nearby Hanbury Street in search of a customer. Some time between 5.30 and 6am she became yet another victim of Jack the Ripper.

Body in a back yard

Her body was discovered in the back yard of number 29 Hanbury Street, Spitalfields, by an elderly resident who immediately ran for help. Inspector Joseph Chandler was summoned from Commercial Street police station and was the first officer to examine the body, together with police surgeon Dr George Bagster Phillips. Both had seen their share of violent murders but neither was prepared for the gratuitous mutilations in evidence that morning.

While neighbours leaned out of their rear windows overlooking the yard, Dr Phillips made an initial examination to determine the time and cause of death. Annie was lying on her back along the fence with her head a few centimetres from the bottom step leading from the back door into the yard. Her blood-smeared hands had stiffened in her death agony as if clutching at her throat, which was wrapped in a handkerchief that the

The final resting place of Annie Chapman

killer might have used to stem the flow of blood, and her legs were drawn up as if she had been having sex when she was killed. The throat had been severed by a ragged cut and the small intestine had been removed and thrown over the right shoulder. Two more portions of the belly wall had been peeled back over the left shoulder and the belly wall with the navel, the womb, the uterus and a portion of the bladder had been removed. Dr Phillips was of the opinion that the killer had a rudimentary grasp of anatomy and that he had used a narrow-bladed knife of 15–20cm (6–8in) in length such as a slaughterman might use – or a surgeon specializing in amputation.

A gruesome search

A search of the yard yielded what appeared to be a number of significant clues, the most promising of which was a wet leather apron hanging a few feet from a dripping tap which it was thought might have been used by the murderer to protect his clothes from being spattered with blood. But inquiries determined that it belonged to the son of one of the residents who had washed it and left it to dry a couple of days earlier. Similarly, a portion of an envelope bearing the seal of the Sussex Regiment and the letters 'M' and 'Sp' looked promising. The envelope contained pills and was postmarked 'London, August 23'. But it too proved a false lead. Witnesses had seen Annie pick up a discarded envelope from the floor of her lodging house which answered the description of the portion found near the body and the pills had been hers.

Perhaps the most curious detail was that her paltry personal possessions – a toothbrush and comb – had been placed on a piece of muslin and neatly arranged at her feet as if part of a bizarre ritual. Or perhaps they had been placed there merely to taunt the police? And then there was the matter of the missing rings. The abrasions on her fingers suggested that they had been wrenched off violently, yet both were clearly imitation gold and worth no more than a few shillings. A thorough search of the local pawn shops failed to locate them. The only possible explanation is that they had been taken by the killer as souvenirs of the kill.

The inhabitants of number 29 and their neighbours wasted no time in exploiting the commercial potential of their location. Even after the body had been taken away they were still charging a penny to view the murder site from their back windows.

In a subsequent editorial *The Times* speculated:

'Intelligent observers who have visited the locality express the utmost astonishment that the murderer could have reached a hiding place after committing such a crime. He must have left the yard in Hanbury Street reeking with blood, and yet, if the theory that the murder took place between 5 and 6

be accepted, he must have walked in almost broad daylight along streets comparatively well frequented, even at that early hour, without his startling appearance attracting the slightest attention.

Consideration of this point has led many to the conclusion that the murderer came not from the wretched class from which the inmates of common lodging-houses are drawn. More probably, it is argued, he is a man lodging in a comparatively decent house in the district, to which he would be able to retire quickly, and in which, once it was reached, he would be able at his leisure to remove from his person all traces of his hideous crime . . . The murderer must have known the neighbourhood, which is provided with no fewer than four police stations, and is well watched nightly, on account of the character of many of the inhabitants.'

Inquest into the death of Annie Chapman

The full extent of the Ripper's rudimentary surgical skills can best be gleaned from evidence given at the inquest into the death of Annie Chapman by Dr George Bagster Phillips, the divisional surgeon of police.

'**Dr Phillips:** *I found the body of the deceased lying in the yard on her back. The face was swollen and turned on the right side, and the tongue protruded between the front teeth, but not beyond* the lips; it was much swollen. The small intestines and other portions were lying on the right side of the body on the ground above the right shoulder, but attached. There was a large quantity of blood, with a part of the stomach above the left shoulder.

The throat was dissevered deeply. I noticed that the incision of the skin was jagged, and reached right round the neck. On the back wall of the house, between the steps and the palings, on the left side, about 18in from the ground, there were about six patches of blood, varying in size from a sixpenny piece to a small point, and on the wooden fence there were smears of blood, corresponding to where the head of the deceased laid, and immediately above the part where the blood had mainly flowed from the neck, which was well clotted.

The incisions of the skin indicated that they had been made from the left side of the neck on a line with the angle of the jaw, carried entirely round and again in front of the neck, and ending at a point about midway between the jaw and the sternum or breast bone on the right hand. There were two distinct clean cuts on the body of the vertebrae on the left side of the spine. They were parallel to each other, and separated by about half an inch. The muscular structures between the side processes of bone of the vertebrae had an appearance as if an attempt had been made to separate the bones of the neck. There are various other mutilations of the body, but I am of opinion that they occurred subsequently to the death of the woman and to the large escape of blood from the neck.

Coroner: Was there any anatomical knowledge displayed?

Dr Phillips: I think there was. There were indications of it. My own impression is that that anatomical knowledge was only less displayed or indicated in consequence of haste. The person evidently was hindered from making a more complete dissection in consequence of the haste.

Coroner: Was the whole of the body there?

Dr Phillips: No; the absent portions being from the abdomen.

Coroner: Are those portions such as would require anatomical knowledge to extract?

Dr Phillips: I think the mode in which they were extracted did show some anatomical knowledge.

Coroner: In your opinion did she enter the yard alive?

Dr Phillips: I am positive of it. I made a thorough search of the passage, and I saw no trace of blood, which must have been visible had she been taken into the yard. I am of opinion that the person who cut the deceased's throat took hold of her by the chin, and then commenced the incision from left to right.

Coroner: Could that be done so instantaneously that a person could not cry out?

Dr Phillips: By pressure on the throat no doubt it would be possible.

Coroner: Can you give any idea how long it would take to perform the incisions found on the body?

Dr Phillips: I think I can guide you by saying that I myself could not have performed all the injuries I saw on that woman, and effect them, even without a struggle, under a quarter of an hour. If I had done it in a deliberate way, such as would fall to the duties of a surgeon, it would probably have taken me the best part of an hour. The whole inference seems to me that the operation was performed to enable the perpetrator to obtain possession of these parts of the body.'

Leather Apron

On 4 September the national newspapers revealed that the police were hunting a vile individual known locally as Leather Apron. He had been brought to the attention of the

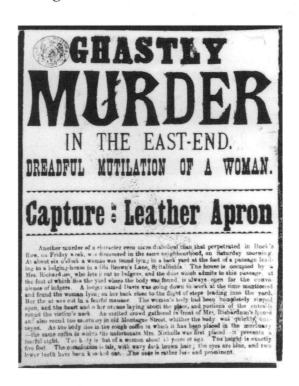

authorities because of his reputation for violent assaults upon prostitutes in the area whom he would threaten with a knife, and if they did not pay him he would beat them until they promised to do so.

His real name was John Pizer but he acquired his nickname from the leather apron he had worn while working as a slipper-maker and which he continued to wear even after he found that extortion was more lucrative.

As soon as Pizer learned that he was being sought in connection with the Whitechapel killings he made himself scarce and it took the police a week to track him down to a relative's house at 22 Mulberry Street.

On 11 September *The Times* reported his arrest, the first in what proved to be a series of false leads that plagued the investigation from the first.

'*Yesterday morning Detective Sergeant Thicke, of the H Division, who has been indefatigable in his inquiries respecting the murder of Annie Chapman at 29, Hanbury Street, Spitalfields, on Saturday morning, succeeded in capturing a man whom he believed to be "Leather Apron." It will be recollected that this person obtained an evil notoriety during the inquiries respecting this and the recent murders committed in Whitechapel, owing to the startling reports that had been freely circulated by many of the women living in the district as to outrages alleged to have been committed by him . . .*

Shortly after 8 o'clock yesterday morning Sergeant Thicke, accompanied by two or three other officers, proceeded to 22, Mulberry Street and knocked at the door. It was opened by a Polish Jew named Pizer, supposed to be "Leather Apron." Thicke at once took hold of the man, saying, "You are just the man I want." He then charged Pizer with being concerned in the murder of the woman Chapman, and to this he made no reply. The accused man, who is a boot finisher by trade, was then handed over to other officers and the house was searched. Thicke took possession of five sharp long-bladed knives – which, however, are used by men in Pizer's trade – and also several old hats. With reference to the latter, several women who stated they were acquainted with the prisoner, alleged he has been in the habit of wearing different hats. Pizer, who is about 33, was then quietly removed to the Leman Street Police station, his friends protesting that he knew nothing of the affair, that he had not been out of the house since Thursday night, and is of a very delicate constitution. The friends of the man were subjected to a close questioning by the police. It was still uncertain, late last night, whether this man remained in custody or had been liberated. He strongly denies that he is known by the name of "Leather Apron."'

Pizer had an alibi for the night Polly Nichols was murdered. He claimed to have been in a lodging house in Holloway Road and his statement was subsequently confirmed by the owner. When Annie Chapman was killed he was in hiding at his brother's house. Nevertheless, he was kept in a cell overnight and included in an identification parade the following day. The only witness was a tramp who swore that Pizer was the man he had seen threatening a woman on the night of the Nichols murder, but on closer questioning the witness proved unreliable and Pizer was released.

The only witness was a tramp... but on closer questioning, the witness proved unreliable

Pizer was ordered to appear before the inquest into the death of Annie Chapman to account for his movements on the night in question and this gave the press their first look at one of Whitechapel's most unsavoury characters. *The East London Observer* described him in Dickensian terms:

'He was a man of about five feet four inches, with a dark-hued face, which was not altogether pleasant to look upon by reason of the grizzly black strips of hair, nearly an inch in length, which almost covered the face. The thin lips, too, had a cruel, sardonic kind of look, which was increased, if anything, by the drooping dark moustache and side whiskers. His hair was short, smooth, and dark, intermingled with grey, and his head was slightly bald on the top. The head was large, and was fixed to the body by a thick heavy-looking neck. Pizer wore a dark overcoat, brown trousers, and a brown and very much battered hat, and appeared somewhat splay-footed.

When Baxter [the Coroner] asked Pizer why he went into hiding after the deaths of Polly Nichols and Annie Chapman, Pizer said that his brother had advised him to do so.

"I was the subject of a false suspicion," he said emphatically.

"It was not the best advice that could be given to you," Baxter returned.

Pizer shot back immediately, "I will tell you why. I should have been torn to pieces!"

'No mere slaughterer of animals'

On 26 September the coroner summed up the evidence, including the eyewitness testimony of a Mrs Long, who may have been the first person to give a description of Jack The Ripper.

'At half-past five, Mrs. Long . . . remembers having seen a man and woman standing a few yards from the place where the deceased is afterwards found. And, although she did not know Annie Chapman, she is positive that that woman was the deceased. The two were talking loudly, but not sufficiently so to arouse her suspicions that there was

anything wrong. Such words as she overheard were not calculated to do so. The laconic inquiry of the man, "Will you?" and the simple assent of the woman, viewed in the light of subsequent events, can be easily translated and explained. Mrs. Long passed on her way, and neither saw nor heard anything more of her, and this is the last time she is known to have been alive.

[Neighbour Albert] Cadosch says it was about 5.20 when he was in the backyard of the adjoining house, and heard a voice say "No," and three or four minutes afterwards a fall against the fence.

The street door and the yard door were never locked, and the passage and yard appear to have been constantly used by people who had no legitimate business there. There is little doubt that the deceased knew the place, for it was only 300 or 400 yards from where she lodged.

The wretch must have then seized the deceased, perhaps with Judas-like approaches. He seized her by the chin. He pressed her throat, and while thus preventing the slightest cry, he at the same time produced insensibility and suffocation. There is no evidence of any struggle. The clothes are not torn. Even in these preliminaries, the wretch seems to have known how to carry out efficiently his nefarious work.

The deceased was then lowered to the ground, and laid on her back; and although in doing so she may have fallen slightly against the fence, this movement was probably effected with care. Her throat was then cut in two places with savage determination, and the injuries to the abdomen commenced. All was done with cool impudence and reckless daring; but, perhaps, nothing is more noticeable than the emptying of her pockets, and the arrangement of their contents with business-like precision in order near her feet. The murder seems, like the Buck's-row case, to have been carried out without any cry. Sixteen people were in the house. The partitions of the different rooms are of wood. None of the occupants of the houses by which the yard is surrounded heard anything suspicious.

The brute who committed the offence did not even take the trouble to cover up his ghastly work, but left the body exposed to the view of the first comer. This accords but little with the trouble taken with the rings, and suggests either that he had at length been disturbed, or

that as the daylight broke a sudden fear suggested the danger of detection that he was running. There are two things missing. Her rings had been wrenched from her fingers and have not been found, and the uterus has been removed. The body has not been dissected, but the injuries have been made by some one who had considerable anatomical skill and knowledge. There are no meaningless cuts. It was done by one who knew where to find what he wanted, what difficulties he would have to contend against, and how he should use his knife, so as to abstract the organ without injury to it. No unskilled person could have known where to find it, or have recognised it when it was found. For instance, no mere slaughterer of animals could have carried out these operations. It must have been some one accustomed to the post-mortem room.

The conclusion that the desire was to possess the missing part seems overwhelming. We are driven to the deduction that the mutilation was the object, and the theft of the rings was only a thin-veiled blind, an attempt to prevent the real intention being discovered. It has been suggested that the criminal is a lunatic with morbid feelings. This may or may not be the case; but the object of the murderer appears palpably shown by the facts, and it is not necessary to assume lunacy, for it is clear that there is a market for the object of the murder.

Within a few hours of the issue of the morning papers containing a report of the medical evidence given at the last

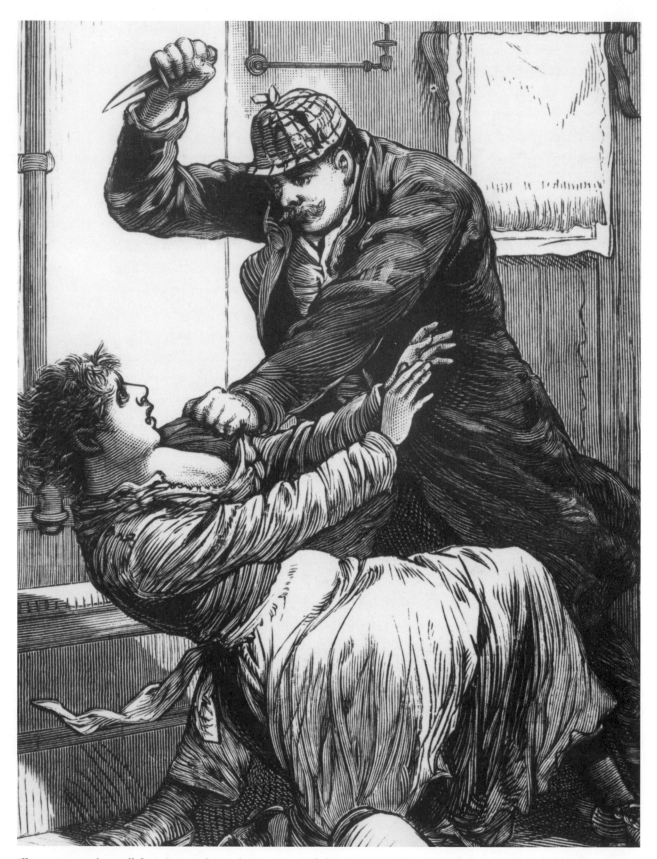

Illustrators made small fortunes supplying their versions of the gruesome killings which further inflated the Ripper myth

sitting of the Court, I received a communication from an officer of one of our great medical schools, that they had information which might or might not have a distinct bearing on our inquiry. I attended at the first opportunity, and was told by the sub-curator of the Pathological Museum that some months ago an American had called on him, and asked him to procure a number of specimens of the organ that was missing in the deceased. He stated his willingness to give £20 for each, and explained that his object was to issue an actual specimen with each copy of a publication on which he was then engaged. Although he was told that his wish was impossible to be complied with, he still urged his request. He desired them preserved, not in spirits of wine, the usual medium, but in glycerine, in order to preserve them in a flaccid condition, and he wished them sent to America direct. It is known that this request was repeated to another institution of a similar character.

It is, therefore, a great misfortune that nearly three weeks have elapsed without the chief actor in this awful tragedy having been discovered. Surely, it is not too much even yet to hope that the ingenuity of our detective force will succeed in unearthing this monster. It is not as if there were no clue to the character of the criminal or the cause of his crime. His object is clearly divulged. His anatomical skill carries him out of the category of a common criminal, for his knowledge could only have been obtained by assisting at post-mortems, or

by frequenting the post-mortem room. If Mrs. Long's memory does not fail, and the assumption be correct that the man who was talking to the deceased at half-past five was the culprit, he is even more clearly defined. In addition to his former description, we should know that he was a foreigner of dark complexion, over forty years of age, a little taller than the deceased, of shabby-genteel appearance, with a brown deer-stalker hat on his head, and a dark coat on his back.'

A verdict of wilful murder against a person or persons unknown was then entered.

It is thought that Mrs Long had formed the impression that Chapman's companion was a foreigner from his accent, as she didn't see his face. For many years this has been understood to mean that he was a European, most likely a Jew, but evidence recently uncovered points to the possibility that he might have been an American, which would tie in with the coroner's story of the doctor who expressed an interest in purchasing anatomical specimens.

A surplus of suspects

Contrary to contemporary public opinion and the claims made by an impatient press, the police made exhaustive inquiries in the area following the murder of Annie Chapman, visiting over 200 common lodging houses and following every single lead offered by anxious residents, all of which led to a dead end. Then, as now, there were people in the habit of making false confessions, either because they were mentally disturbed or because they were seeking attention. And, of course, there were many false and malicious claims made against innocent people which the police were obliged to investigate.

During September Sir Charles Warren came under increasing pressure from the Home Office, which wanted assurances that the police would be making an imminent arrest. In an effort to placate them, he submitted a confidential report in which he detailed the individuals currently under suspicion.

'No progress has yet been made in obtaining any definite clue to the Whitechapel murderers. A great number of clues have been examined and exhausted without finding anything suspicious. A large staff of men are employed and every point is being examined which seems to offer any prospect of a discovery.

There are at present three cases of suspicion.

1. The lunatic Isensmith [sic], a Swiss arrested at Holloway who is now in an asylum at Bow and arrangements are being made to ascertain whether he is the man who was seen on the morning of the murder in a public house by Mrs Fiddymont.

2. A man called Puckeridge was released from an asylum on 4 August. He was

educated as a surgeon and has threatened to rip people up with a long knife. He is being looked for but cannot be found as yet.

3. A Brothel Keeper who will not give her address or name writes to say that a man living in her house was seen with blood on him on the morning of murder. She described his appearance and said where he might be seen. When the detectives came near he bolted, got away and there is no clue to the writer of the letter.

All these three cases are being followed up and no doubt will be exhausted in a few days – the first seems a very suspicious case, but the man is at present a violent lunatic.'

Of the three suspects, Isenschmid seemed the most likely perpetrator at the time. He had been arrested on 12 September after two doctors and the landlady of a public house had reported his eccentric and threatening behaviour to the police. Dr Cowan and Dr Crabb informed the authorities that in their professional opinion Isenschmid was a violent lunatic and that he disappeared from his lodgings at odd hours of the night. He was also known to have a habit of sharpening knives in the vicinity of anyone he didn't like the look of, as if to intimidate them. Four days earlier, on the morning of the Chapman murder, Mrs Fiddymout, the landlady of the Prince Albert public house, had been disturbed by the appearance of a furtive man who had a wild look in his

Light was thrown into many dark corners, but try as they might the Metropolitan Police could not pin down the Ripper

eyes and dried blood on his hands. It was Isenschmid, but his brother supplied an alibi for his movements on the day of the Chapman murder and he was released after the Ripper struck again while he was still under arrest.

Oswald Puckridge still looks like a viable suspect, although he was 50 years old at the time of the Ripper murders, which does not conform with the eye-witness descriptions. He was released from Hoxton House Lunatic Asylum three days before Martha Tabram was murdered and he ended his days in Holborn Workhouse on 28 May 1900, so he was at large during the crucial period. However, there is no evidence of any kind to connect him with the killings.

The third man referred to in Warren's report was probably Francis Tumblety, an American doctor, who, in the light of recently uncovered evidence, now seems a very likely candidate for the Whitechapel murders (see page 137).

An unfortunate double event – 30 September 1888

'Long Liz' was comparatively fortunate in that she was spared the ghastly mutilations which the Whitechapel fiend had inflicted on the other women and was instead despatched with a single slice of a razor-sharp blade. However, for this reason there is still some doubt that she was an 'official' Ripper victim, but may have been slain by another hand.

In all other respects her story was much like the other women.

A farmer's daughter and Swedish by birth, Elizabeth Stride had left her home country in 1866 and emigrated to England after the death of her parents and the trauma of having given birth to a stillborn baby. Her marriage to carpenter John Stride did not last long and she was soon walking the streets of Whitechapel. On the night of her death, in the early hours of 30 September 1888, she had been working as a cleaner in Flower And Dean Street but needed to supplement her pitiable income by prostitution.

By all accounts she was slim and pretty, a more attractive prospect than the dowdy bawds with whom she shared a pitch, and she had made an effort to make herself presentable for the punters. To her long, black, fur-trimmed jacket she had pinned a red rose, which proved an important detail when it came to establishing her movements and the veracity of the various conflicting witness statements. In addition she was wearing a black crêpe bonnet, a dark threadbare skirt, a brown bodice, white stockings and the customary side-spring boots.

It was the rose which helped PC William Smith to be confident that it was Stride he had seen with a man in Berner Street 30 minutes after midnight. Her companion was 170cm (5ft 7in) tall, of respectable appearance, and carried a small parcel wrapped in newspaper which the constable

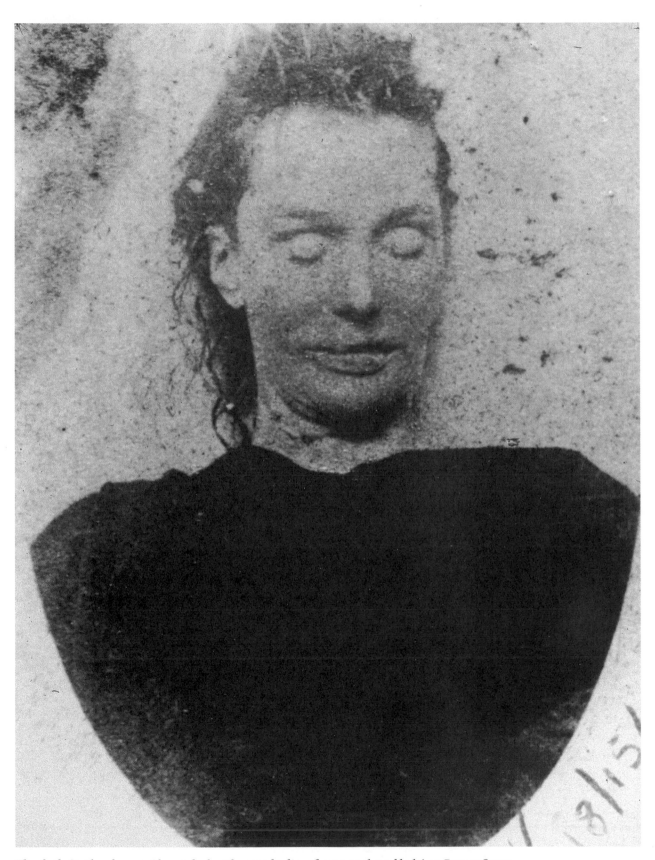

Elizabeth Stride who was 'despatched with a single slice of a razor-sharp blade' on Berner Street

estimated was 15–20cm (6–8in) broad and about 45cm (18in) long – the right size to contain a small medical bag, perhaps? He was about 28 years of age, with a dark complexion and a small dark moustache, and was wearing a dark coat, dark trousers, white collar and tie and a hard felt deerstalker hat of the kind made famous by Sherlock Holmes.

A second witness

Fifteen minutes later Israel Schwartz, a Hungarian Jewish immigrant who spoke little English, witnessed a struggle at the very spot where Stride's body was later found, by the gate to Dutfield's Yard in Berner Street. The man was attempting to drag the woman into the street, then threw her to the ground whereupon she screamed. Frightened of becoming involved in a violent argument, Schwartz crossed over the road, passing a second man who was lighting his pipe. A moment later the first man called out 'Lipski!' (a derogatory generic name for a Jew, deriving from the name of a notorious murderer who was still in the public mind at that time), whereupon the pipe-smoker gave chase and Schwartz fled, fearing for his life.

After evading his pursuer Schwartz reported the incident to the police and gave the following descriptions of the two men, neither of whom conforms to the descriptions of previous suspects. The man who assaulted the woman was approximately 165cm (5ft 5in) tall, round-faced and broad-shouldered, with dark hair and a short brown moustache. He was wearing a dark jacket and trousers and a dark peaked cap. Schwartz thought he might have been about 30 years of age. The man with the pipe was in his mid-thirties, 180cm (5ft 11in) tall, with light brown hair, and was wearing a dark overcoat and a black wide-brimmed hat.

Was it the Ripper?

A possible explanation for the incident might be that the first man took exception to a stranger – particularly a Jew – being a witness to his argument with the woman and may have ordered his friend to give chase. This second sighting is the more intriguing as it places Stride at the murder scene just 15 minutes before her death and raises the distinct possibility that she was murdered by the men Schwartz saw and not the Ripper. This would explain why there were no post-mortem mutilations. And then there is the testimony of Dr Phillips, the police surgeon, who told the Stride inquest on 1 October that there was a 'great dissimilarity' between the Chapman and Stride murders, specifically the choice of weapon, which was a round-bladed knife in the latter case. This raises the possibility that Stride may have been murdered by her brutal former partner Michael Kidney, from whom she had separated only a few days earlier, and that Kidney was the man Schwartz had seen pushing her to the ground.

However, many Ripper historians disagree, arguing that Stride had still 15 minutes to meet her murderer after the two thugs had moved on and that the reason for the lack of mutilations was that the Ripper was interrupted by the arrival of a hawker, Louis Diemschutz, who pulled into Dutfield's Yard in his pony and trap at 1am. When the horse shied Diemschutz looked to see what had disturbed it and saw what appeared to be a bundle of clothes on the ground. But it was too dark to see clearly. The only light in the yard came from the windows of a socialist club to the right and from the second-storey windows of the tenement opposite. The fitful light from the street lamp outside was not strong enough to illuminate the yard even though Diemschutz had left the gate wide open. So he prodded the bundle with his whip and then lit a match which blew out in the wind – but the brief glimpse he caught was enough for him to see that it was a woman's body. Her throat had been slit, the windpipe severed, the blood clotting a cheap check scarf around her neck. She was lying on her left side with her legs drawn up, knees together. In her left hand she clutched a packet of cheap breath fresheners, the contents of which had rolled into the gutter. Her right hand lay across her stomach, speckled with blood.

> *Her throat had been slit, the windpipe severed, the blood clotting a cheap scarf around her neck*

The body of Elizabeth Stride was still warm when Dr Frederick Blackwell examined it at the site just after 1.15am, which suggested that she had been killed between 12.45am and 1am when Diemschutz entered the yard. If he had disturbed the Ripper in the act then the killer's bloodlust must have been unsatisfied and it would explain why he took such pitiless revenge on his second victim of the night, Catherine Eddowes.

Inquest into the death of Elizabeth Stride

On the first day of the inquest into the death of Elizabeth Stride on 2 October 1888, Dr George Bagster Phillips testified:

'On Oct. 1, at three p.m., at St. George's Mortuary, Dr. Blackwell and I made a post-mortem examination, Dr. Blackwell kindly consenting to make the dissection, and I took the following note:

"Rigor mortis still firmly marked. Mud on face and left side of the head. Matted on the hair and left side. We removed the clothes. We found the body fairly nourished. Over both shoulders, especially the right, from the front aspect under collar bones and in front of chest

there is a bluish discolouration which I have watched and seen on two occasions since. On neck, from left to right, there is a clean cut incision six inches in length; incision commencing two and a half inches in a straight line below the angle of the jaw. Three-quarters of an inch over undivided muscle, then becoming deeper, about an inch dividing sheath and the vessels, ascending a little, and then grazing the muscle outside the cartilages on the left side of the neck. The carotid artery on the left side and the other vessels contained in the sheath were all cut through, save the posterior portion of the carotid, to a line about 1-12th of an inch in extent, which prevented the separation of the upper and lower portion of the artery. The cut through the tissues on the right side of the cartilages is more superficial, and tails off to about two inches below the right angle of the jaw. It is evident that the haemorrhage which produced death was caused through the partial severance of the left carotid artery . . .

I have come to a conclusion as to the position of both the murderer and the victim, and I opine that the latter was seized by the shoulders and placed on the ground, and that the murderer was on her right side when he inflicted the cut. I am of opinion that the cut was made from the left to the right side of the deceased, and taking into account the position of the incision it is unlikely that [...] a long knife inflicted the wound in the neck.

Coroner: *From the position you assume the perpetrator to have been in, would he*

have been likely to get bloodstained?

Dr Phillips: *Not necessarily, for the commencement of the wound and the injury to the vessels would be away from him, and the stream of blood – for stream it was – would be directed away from him, and towards the gutter in the yard.*

Coroner: *But why did she not cry out while she was being put on the ground?*

Dr Phillips: *She was in a yard, and in a locality where she might cry out very loudly and no notice be taken of her. It was possible for the woman to draw up her legs after the wound, but she could not have turned over. The wound was inflicted by drawing the knife across the throat. A short knife, such as a shoemaker's well-ground knife, would do the same thing. My reason for believing that deceased was injured when on the ground was partly on account of the absence of blood anywhere on the left side of the body and between it and the wall.'*

At the close of the inquest Dr Blackwell was called to give evidence and, asked by the foreman of the jury if he had noticed any marks or bruises about the shoulders, replied, 'They were what we call pressure marks. At first they were very obscure, but subsequently they became very evident. They were not what are ordinarily called bruises; neither is there any abrasion. Each shoulder was about equally marked.'

In summing up on the final day the coroner attempted to clarify the apparently conflicting testimony of three key witnesses who claimed to have seen a woman answering the description of the deceased in the company of a man near the location where the body was discovered between 15 minutes and an hour later.

'William Marshall, who lived at 64, Berner-street, was standing at his doorway from half-past 11 till midnight. About a quarter to 12 o'clock he saw the deceased talking to a man between Fairclough-street and Boyd-street. There was every demonstration of affection by the man during the ten minutes they stood together, and when last seen, strolling down the road towards Ellen Street, his arms were round her neck.

At 12 30 p.m. the constable on the beat (William Smith) saw the deceased in Berner Street standing on the pavement a few yards from Commercial-street, and he observed she was wearing a flower in her dress.

WHERE THE CORPSE WAS FOUND IN BERNERS STREET.

Artistically framed sketch of the murder scene

A quarter of an hour afterwards James Brown, of Fairclough-street, passed the deceased close to the Board school. A man was at her side leaning against the wall, and the deceased was heard to say, "Not to-night, but some other night." Now, if this evidence was to be relied on, it would appear that the deceased was in the company of a man for upwards of an hour immediately before her death, and that within a quarter of an hour of her being found a corpse she was refusing her companion something in the immediate neighbourhood of where she met her death. But was this the deceased? And even if it were, was it one and the same man who was seen in her company on three different occasions?

With regard to the identity of the woman, Marshall had the opportunity of watching her for ten minutes while standing talking in the street at a short distance from him, and she afterwards passed close to him. The constable feels certain that the woman he observed was the deceased, and when he afterwards was called to the scene of the crime he at once recognized her and made a statement; while Brown was almost certain that the deceased was the woman to whom his attention was attracted. It might be thought that the frequency of the occurrence of men and women being seen together under similar

A man was at her side leaning against the wall and the deceased was heard to say, 'Not to-night, but some other night'

circumstances might have led to mistaken identity; but the police stated, and several of the witnesses corroborated the statement, that although many couples are to be seen at night in the Commercial-road, it was exceptional to meet them in Berner Street.

With regard to the man seen, there were many points of similarity, but some of dissimilarity, in the descriptions of the three witnesses; but these discrepancies did not conclusively prove that there was more than one man in the company of the deceased, for every day's experience showed how facts were differently observed and differently described by honest and intelligent witnesses. Brown, who saw least in consequence of the darkness of the spot at which the two were standing, agreed with Smith that his clothes were dark and that his height was about 5ft. 7in., but he appeared to him to be wearing an overcoat nearly down to his heels; while the description of Marshall accorded with that of Smith in every respect but two. They agreed that he was respectably dressed in a black cut away coat and dark trousers, and that he was of middle age and without whiskers.

On the other hand, they differed with regard to what he was wearing on his head. Smith stated he wore a hard felt deer stalker of dark colour; Marshall that he was wearing a round cap with a *small peak, like a sailor's. They also differed as to whether he had anything in his hand. Marshall stated that he observed nothing. Smith was very precise, and stated that he was carrying a parcel, done up in a newspaper, about 18in. in length and 6in. to 8in. in width. These differences suggested either that the woman was, during the evening, in the company of more than one man – a not very improbable supposition – or that the witness had been mistaken in detail. If they were correct in assuming that the man seen in the company of the deceased by the three was one and the same person it followed that he must have spent much time and trouble to induce her to place herself in his diabolical clutches.*

In the absence of motive, the age and class of woman selected as victim, and the place and time of the crime, there was a similarity between this case and those mysteries which had recently occurred in that neighbourhood. There had been no skilful mutilation as in the cases of Nichols and Chapman, and no unskilful injuries as in the case in Mitre Square [see page 62], possibly the work of an imitator; but there had been the same skill exhibited in the way in which the victim had been entrapped, and the injuries inflicted, so as to cause instant death and prevent blood from soiling the operator, and the same daring defiance of immediate detection, which, unfortunately for the peace of the inhabitants and trade of the neighbourhood, had hitherto been only too successful.'

After a short deliberation the jury returned a verdict of 'Wilful murder against some person or persons unknown' and the inquest into the death of Long Liz was concluded.

Murder in Mitre Square

Forty-six-year-old Catherine Eddowes had not entirely slept off her drink when her cell door was opened at 12.55am and she was ushered on her way by the jailer at Bishopsgate police station. She had been singing softly to herself for almost an hour and was deemed sufficiently sober to be released. 'I am capable of taking care of myself now,' she assured PC Hutt, the duty officer, as she made her way unsteadily towards the exit at the end of a passage. Then she enquired, 'What time is it?' PC Hutt replied it was just before one and too late for her to get any more drink, to which Eddowes responded, 'I shall get a fine hiding when I get home, then.'

'Serves you right,' said the PC as he watched her cross the station yard, adding that he would be obliged if she could close the back door on her way out. 'All right,' she replied. 'Good night, old cock.'

It was beginning to rain as she turned down Houndsditch toward Aldgate High Street, but her black straw bonnet would keep her hair from getting bedraggled. She wore a black cloth jacket trimmed with imitation fur, a brown bodice and a green alpaca skirt with a white apron, which gave

Bishopsgate Street, as portrayed by Gustave Doré, was typical of London's many bustling slums

her an appearance more in keeping with a charwoman than a streetwalker.

Eight minutes later she entered Mitre Square, a gloomy, ill-lit quadrangle bounded on all sides by grim, imposing warehouses. About 20 minutes later PC Watkins crossed the square, shining his bull's-eye lamp into the dark recesses of the quadrangle and, seeing nothing unusual, he continued on his beat, which took 12–14 minutes to complete. Had he not stopped for a cup of tea offered by a night watchman he might have caught the Ripper in the act.

Another body found

At 1.35am three men, Joseph Lawende, Joseph Levy and Harry Harris, passed a couple taking shelter at the corner of Church Passage which led into the square. Lawende did not see the woman's face as she had her back to him and could only describe her as being short. She was wearing a black bonnet and a jacket of the same colour. It is likely that it was Catherine Eddowes and that her companion was her murderer. She had her hand on his chest, indicative of intimacy, and they were conversing quietly. Lawende caught only a glimpse of the man who he later described as 'rough and shabby', aged about 30, approximately 165cm (5ft 7in) tall and of medium build with a fair complexion and a fair moustache. He was wearing a grey peaked cloth cap and a pepper and salt-coloured jacket with a reddish handkerchief tied around his neck. But it was such a fleeting glimpse that Lawende later admitted to the police that he would not be confident of recognizing the man if he ever came face to face with him. His friends could add nothing to the description, although Levy observed that the couple were rum-looking characters who made him uncomfortable and that he was glad not to be walking alone in that area at night.

Ten minutes later PC Watkins had completed his circuit and returned to Mitre Square. In the south-western corner he came upon the body of Catherine Eddowes 'ripped open, like a pig in the market'. Her horrifying mutilations sickened even the seasoned City of London Police surgeon, Dr Brown, who was summoned to the scene at 2am.

'The body was on its back,' he noted. 'The clothes [were] drawn up above the abdomen, the thighs were naked . . . the abdomen was exposed . . . great disfigurement of [the] face, the throat cut across . . .

'The intestines were drawn out to a large extent and placed over the right shoulder – they were smeared over with some feculent matter, a piece [of] about two feet were quite detached from the body and placed between the body and the left arm, apparently by design. The lobe and auricle of the right ear was cut obliquely through . . . There were no traces of recent connection.'

When the body arrived at the

mortuary a piece of her ear fell from the clothing in which it had been caught. During the post-mortem Dr Brown elaborated on the bizarre facial mutilations he had previously referred to.

'There was a cut above a quarter of an inch through the lower left eyelid dividing the structures completely through. The upper eyelid on that side, there was a scratch through the skin on the left upper eyelid near to the angle of the nose. The right eyelid was cut through to half an inch. There was a deep cut over the bridge of the nose extending from the left border of the nasal bone down near to the angle of the jaw on the right side across the cheek, this cut went into the bone and divided all the structures of the cheek except the mucous membrane of the mouth. The tip of the nose was quite detached from the [rest of] the nose by an oblique cut from the bottom of the nasal bone to where the wings of the nose join on to the face . . . There was on each side of [the] cheek a cut which peeled up the skin forming a triangular flap about an inch and a half.'

The inquest

At the inquest on Thursday, 4 October, Dr Brown was asked to give details regarding the missing organs, and reported, 'The uterus was cut away with the exception of a small portion, and the left kidney was also cut out. Both these organs were absent, and have not been found.' The coroner then asked if he had any opinion as to what position the woman was in when the wounds were inflicted:

*'**Dr Brown:** In my opinion the woman must have been lying down. The way in which the kidney was cut out showed that it was done by somebody who knew what he was about.'*
__Coroner:__ Does the nature of the wounds lead you to any conclusion as to the instrument that was used?
__Dr Brown:__ It must have been a sharp-pointed knife, and I should say at least 6 in. long.
__Coroner:__ Would you consider that the person who inflicted the wounds possessed anatomical skill?
__Dr Brown:__ He must have had a good deal of knowledge as to the position of the abdominal organs, and the way to remove them.
__Coroner:__ Would the removal of the kidney, for example, require special knowledge?
__Dr Brown:__ It would require a good deal of knowledge as to its position, because it is apt to be overlooked, being covered by a membrane.
__Coroner:__ Would such a knowledge be likely to be possessed by some one accustomed to cutting up animals?
__Dr Brown:__ Yes.
__Coroner:__ Have you been able to form any opinion as to whether the perpetrator of this act was disturbed?
__Dr Brown:__ I think he had sufficient time, but it was in all probability done in a hurry.

Kate Eddowes.

Horribly mutilated: Catherine Eddowes was murdered in Mitre Square, a gloomy ill-lit quadrangle bounded by warehouses

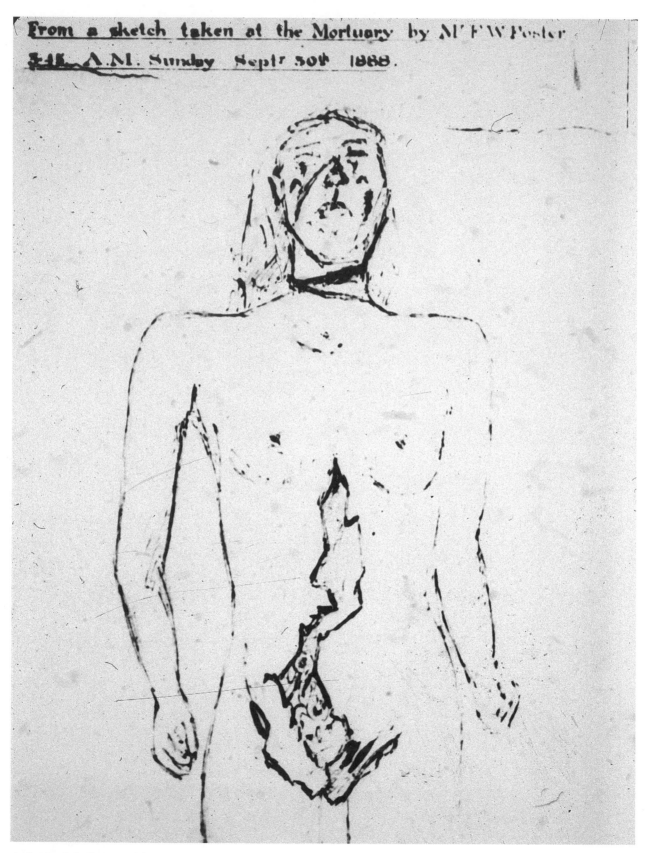

From a sketch taken at the Mortuary by Mr F W Foster 3.45 A.M. Sunday Sept 30th 1888.

A sketch of Catherine Eddowes showing pre- and post-mortem injuries: a piece of her ear fell off in the mortuary

Coroner: How long would it take to make the wounds?

Dr Brown: It might be done in five minutes. It might take him longer; but that is the least time it could be done in.

Coroner: Have you any doubt in your own mind whether there was a struggle?

Dr Brown: I feel sure there was no struggle. I see no reason to doubt that it was the work of one man.

Coroner: Would you expect to find much blood on the person inflicting these wounds?

Dr Brown: No, I should not. I should say that the abdominal wounds were inflicted by a person kneeling at the right side of the body.'

Dr Brown was then asked if it was possible for the deceased to have been murdered elsewhere, and her body brought to where it was found:

'Dr Brown: I do not think there is any foundation for such a theory. The blood on the left side was clotted, and must have fallen at the time the throat was cut. I do not think that the deceased moved the least bit after that.

Coroner: The body could not have been carried to where it was found?

Dr Brown: Oh, no.'

However, Dr Brown's opinion was later contested by Dr G W Sequeira, who had been the first medical man on the scene that night, arriving at 1.55am, no more than 15 minutes after the murder had taken place. 'I think that the murderer had no design on any particular organ of the body,' he declared emphatically. 'He was not possessed of any great anatomical skill.'

The Goulston Street graffiti

'The Juwes are the men that will not be blamed for nothing.' No one knows for certain if the writing found chalked on a wall in Goulston Street on the night of the double murder was a cryptic clue, or if it was merely a coincidence that a portion of Catherine Eddowes' blood-spattered apron was found nearby. The bloodied piece of apron had been spotted at 2.55am by PC Alfred Long who, knowing of the murder in nearby Mitre Square, immediately realized its significance. While searching the immediate vicinity for other possible evidence he noticed the writing and made a note of it. The apron was lying in the passage of what was known as a model dwelling house near to the staircase leading up to Nos. 106 to 119. Long was certain it had not been there when he had passed that way on his previous round at 2.20am.

Detective Daniel Halse of the City Police elaborated on the find at the Catherine Eddowes inquest:

'On Saturday, Sept. 29 [sic]. . . I proceeded to Goulston Street, where I saw some chalk-writing on the black fascia of the wall. Instructions were given to have the writing photographed,

but before it could be done the Metropolitan police stated that they thought the writing might cause a riot or outbreak against the Jews, and it was decided to have it rubbed out, as the people were already bringing out their stalls into the street.

Coroner: Did the writing have the appearance of having been recently done?

Detective Halse: Yes. It was written with white chalk on a black fascia.

Foreman of the Jury: Why was the writing really rubbed out?

Detective Halse: The Metropolitan police said it might create a riot, and it was their ground.

Coroner: I am obliged to ask this question. Did you protest against the writing being rubbed out?

Detective Halse: I did. I asked that it might, at all events, be allowed to remain until Major Smith [acting Commissioner] had seen it.

Coroner: Why do you say that it seemed to have been recently written?

Detective Halse: It looked fresh, and if it had been done long before it would have been rubbed out by the people passing. I did not notice whether there was any powdered chalk on the ground, though I did look about to see if a knife could be found. There were three lines of writing in a good schoolboy's round hand. The size of the capital letters would be about 3/4 in, and the other letters were in proportion. The writing was on the black bricks, which formed a kind of dado, the bricks above being white.'

No clues in the chalk

Much has been made of the writing and the possible significance of the misspelling of the word Jews, which may or may not have been intentional. In *Jack The Ripper: The Final Solution*, author Stephen Knight spun a convoluted conspiracy theory concerning three mythical founders of the Freemasons known as the Juwes, which was subsequently revealed to have been inspired by an after-dinner story conceived in a moment of mischievous fun by the painter Walter Sickert and to have no basis in fact.

It seems fanciful in the extreme to presume that a serial killer would stalk the streets armed with a piece of chalk in the hope of finding a suitable surface on which to scrawl a provocative message – or that he would have paused to write anything that was not either a direct challenge to the police or in praise of his own audacity. If he was inclined to bravado it is much more likely that he would have written something where the murder had been committed. And if he had written anything to taunt the police he would have dropped the bloodied chalk at the spot so that they would know that it was from the killer. Only an innocent would take the chalk away with them to use on another occasion.

Warren's report to the Home Secretary, 6 November

Sir Charles Warren came under intense public criticism for having authorized the eradication of the Goulston Street graffiti and was forced to justify his action in a report to the Home Secretary.

Confidential
The Under Secretary of State
The Home Office

Sir,
In reply to your letter of the 5th instant, I enclose a report of the circumstances of the Mitre Square Murder so far as they have come under the notice of the Metropolitan Police, and I now give an account regarding the erasing of the writing on the wall in Goulston Street which I have already partially explained to Mr. Matthews verbally.

On the 30th September on hearing of the Berner Street murder, after visiting Commercial Street Station I arrived at Leman Street Station shortly before 5 A.M. and ascertained from the Superintendent Arnold all that was known there relative to the two murders.

The most pressing question at that moment was some writing on the wall in Goulston Street evidently written with the intention of inflaming the public mind against the Jews, and which Mr. Arnold with a view to prevent serious disorder proposed to obliterate, and had sent down an Inspector with a sponge for that purpose, telling him to await his arrival.

I considered it desirable that I should decide the matter myself, as it was one involving so great a responsibility whether any action was taken or not.

I accordingly went down to Goulston Street at once before going to the scene of the murder: it was just getting light, the public would be in the streets in a few minutes, in a neighbourhood very much crowded on Sunday mornings by Jewish vendors and Christian purchasers from all parts of London.

There were several Police around the spot when I arrived, both Metropolitan and City.

The writing was on the jamb of the

As Sir Charles Warren at the Demonstration went back to the chimney-pot hat, are we to infer that he hankers after the old Peeler costume?

Caricature of the head of the Met, from 1888

open archway or doorway visible in the street and could not be covered up without danger of the covering being torn off at once.

A discussion took place whether the writing could be left covered up or otherwise or whether any portion of it could be left for an hour until it could be photographed; but after taking into consideration the excited state of the population in London generally at the time, the strong feeling which had been excited against the Jews, and the fact that in a short time there would be a large concourse of the people in the streets, and having before me the Report that if it was left there the house was likely to be wrecked (in which from my own observation I entirely concurred) I considered it desirable to obliterate the writing at once, having taken a copy of which I enclose a duplicate.

After having been to the scene of the murder, I went on to the City Police Office and informed the Chief Superintendent of the reason why the writing had been obliterated.

I may mention that so great was the feeling with regard to the Jews that on the 13th ulto. the Acting Chief Rabbi wrote to me on the subject of the spelling of the word "Jewes" on account of a newspaper asserting that this was Jewish spelling in the Yiddish dialect. He added "in the present state of excitement it is dangerous to the safety of the poor Jews in the East [End] to allow such an assertion to remain un-contradicted. My community keenly appreciates your humane and vigilant action during this critical time."

It may be realised therefore if the safety of the Jews in Whitechapel could be considered to be jeopardised 13 days after the murder by the question of the spelling of the word Jews, what might have happened to the Jews in that quarter had that writing been left intact.

I do not hesitate myself to say that if that writing had been left there would have been an onslaught upon the Jews, property would have been wrecked, and lives would probably have been lost; and I was much gratified with the promptitude with which Superintendent Arnold was prepared to act in the matter if I had not been there.

I have no doubt myself whatever that

Portrait of Jewish butchers from Aldgate

one of the principal objects of the Reward offered by Mr. Montagu was to show to the world that the Jews were desirous of having the Hanbury Street Murder cleared up, and thus to divert from them the very strong feeling which was then growing up.

I am, Sir,

Your most obedient Servant,

(signed) C. Warren

Two copies of the graffiti were enclosed and read as follows:

The Jewes are
The men that
Will not be
Blamed
for nothing

On the Ripper's trail

In his autobiography *From Constable to Commissioner* (1910), Acting Commissioner of the London Police Sir Henry Smith boasted that 'There is no man living who knows as much of those [Whitechapel] murders as I do.' Among his colleagues Sir Henry enjoyed a reputation as a raconteur who was not above embellishing the truth if it made for a more thrilling yarn. Nevertheless his account of the night of the double murder evokes the atmosphere and urgency of what it was like to have been on the trail of the Ripper.

'In August, 1888, when I was desperately keen to lay my hands on the murderer, I made such arrangements as I thought would insure success. I put nearly a third of the force into plain clothes, with instructions to do everything which, under ordinary circumstances, a constable should not do. It was subversive of discipline; but I had them well supervised by senior officers. The weather was lovely, and I have little doubt they thoroughly enjoyed themselves, sitting on door-steps, smoking their pipes, hanging about public-houses, and gossiping with all and sundry.

In addition to this, I visited every butcher's shop in the city, and every nook and corner which might, by any possibility, be the murderer's place of concealment. Did he live close to the scene of action? Or did he, after committing a murder, make his way with lightning speed to some retreat in the suburbs? Did he carry something with him to wipe the blood from his hands, or did he find means of washing them? were questions I asked myself nearly every hour of the day. It seemed impossible he could be living in the very midst of us; and, seeing the Metropolitan Police had orders to stop every man walking or driving late at night or in the early morning, till he gave a satisfactory account of himself, more impossible still that he could gain Leytonstone, Highgate, Finchley, Fulham, or any suburban district without being arrested. The murderer very soon showed his contempt for my elaborate arrangements. The excitement

The beggars of Orange Court, off Drury Lane

had toned down a little, and I was beginning to think he had either gone abroad or retired from business, when "Two more women murdered in the East!" raised the excitement again to concert pitch.

Jumping up, I was dressed and in the street in a couple of minutes. A hansom – to me a detestable vehicle – was at the door, and into it I jumped, as time was of the utmost consequence. This invention of the devil claims to be safe. It is neither safe nor pleasant . . . it did not take me long to discover that a 15-stone Superintendent inside with me, and three detectives hanging on behind, added neither to its comfort nor to its safety . . . we got to our destination – Mitre Square – without an upset, where I found a small group of my men standing round the mutilated remains of a woman.

It was in Berners Street, a narrow thoroughfare off the Commercial Road leading to the London, Tilbury, and Southend Railway, that Elizabeth Stride, the first of the two victims that night, met her fate. The street is entered by a large wooden gate, folding back in the middle, and almost always left open, and it is conjectured that the murderer took the woman in, closing the gate behind him. At 12.40 a.m., as far as could be made out from the evidence of the inmates, the street was vacant.

Within five minutes of that time a man who had been out late opened the gate. He was driving a pony-trap. The pony shied at something behind the gate,

EXTERIOR OF THE GATE

THE FIFTH VICTIM OF THE WHITECHAPEL FIEND.

and looking down he saw the body of a woman, and instantly gave the alarm. The woman was seriously injured about the head, and must have been thrown down with great violence, and her throat was cut from ear to ear. Not a sound was heard by anyone. No doubt she was rendered insensible by the fall. The assassin must have slipped past the off-side of the pony, and – as there were civilians and some men of the H Division close at hand – escaped by a very hair's-breadth, an experience sufficient, one would have thought, to shake his nerve for that night. But no, either because he was dissatisfied with his work, or furious at having been interrupted before he could finish it, he

determined to show that he was still without a rival as a slaughterer, and, walking straight up to Houndsditch, he met Catherine Eddowes, and finished his second victim within the hour. The approaches to Mitre Square are three – by Mitre Street, Duke Street, and St. James's Place. In the south-western corner, to which there is no approach, lay the woman. I was convinced then, and am convinced now, that had my orders been carried out in the spirit – they may have been to the letter – the reign of terror would have ceased that night . . .

The "beat" of Catherine Eddowes was a small one. She was known to a good many of the constables, but, known or not known, she was in the streets late at

Police sketch of the crime scene at Mitre Square

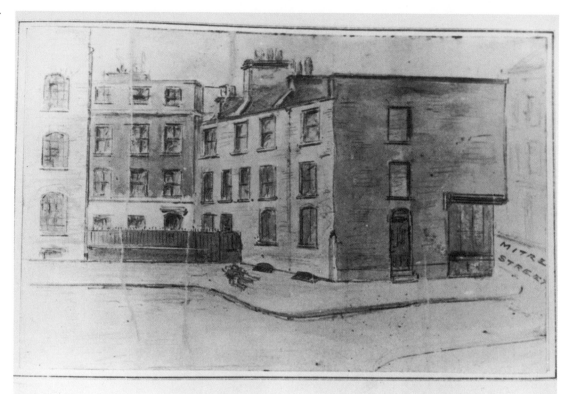

Sketch taken from point B. on plan looking towards A.

night, and must have been seen making for Mitre Square. With what object? In pursuance, it is needless to say, of her miserable calling. Had she been followed, and men called to guard the approaches, the murderer would to a certainty have been taken red-handed. The Square, every inch of it, was carefully examined, but not one mark or drop of blood did we discover to indicate by what approach he had made his exit.

By this time a stretcher had arrived, and when we got the body to the mortuary, the first discovery we made was that about one-half of the apron was missing. It had been severed by a clean cut . . . The assassin had evidently wiped his hands with the piece of apron. In Dorset Street, with extraordinary

audacity, he washed them at a sink up a close, not more than six yards from the street. I arrived there in time to see the blood-stained water. I wandered round my stationhouses, hoping I might find someone brought in, and finally got to bed at 6 a.m., after a very harassing night, completely defeated.

The revolting details of this murder would shock my readers; but there are certain facts – gruesome enough in all conscience – which have never appeared in print, and which, from a medical and scientific point of view, should certainly be put on record.

When the body was examined by the police surgeon, Mr. Gordon Brown, one kidney was found to be missing, and some days after the murder what *purported to be that kidney was posted to the office of the Central News, together with a short note of rather a jocular character unfit for publication. Both kidney and note the manager at once forwarded to me. Unfortunately, as always happens, some clerk or assistant in the office was got at, and the whole affair was public property next morning . . .*

I made over the kidney to the police surgeon, instructing him to consult with the most eminent men in the profession, and send me a report without delay. I give the substance of it. The renal artery is about three inches long. Two inches remained in the corpse, one inch was attached to the kidney.

The kidney left in the corpse was in an advanced stage of Bright's Disease; the kidney sent me was in an exactly similar state. But what was of far more importance, Mr. Sutton . . . one of the greatest authorities living on the kidney and its diseases, said he would pledge his reputation that the kidney submitted to them had been put in spirits within a few hours of its removal from the body – thus effectually disposing of all hoaxes in connection with it. The body of anyone done to death by violence is not taken direct to the dissecting-room, but must await an inquest, never held before the following day at the soonest.

The Ripper certainly had all the luck.'

Interval before the final act

Following the double murder of 30 September, the streets of Whitechapel were uncommonly quiet after dark. Residents complained that after the pubs closed the number of plain-clothes police on the streets and roughs who had been armed with clubs by the Mile End Vigilance Committee outnumbered the inhabitants.

Contrary to public opinion, the police were tireless in their efforts to apprehend the fiend. Almost 100 butchers and slaughtermen were interviewed, as well as dozens of Thames River boatmen. In addition 80,000 handbills appealing for civic-minded individuals to report their suspicions were distributed in the locality.

The newspapers were bombarded with advice from the public on how to catch the killer, which ranged from dressing boxers in women's clothes to act as bait to employing clairvoyants as psychic bloodhounds. Other readers wrote in with their suspicions regarding their neighbours, lodgers and anyone they might have had a grudge against. One particular report, published in the *Star* on 1 October, sounded promising, but nothing more was heard of the man at the centre of this allegation.

'A reporter heard a strange story this morning that may be connected with the murders. A gentleman living not far from the British Museum says: – In the room above mine there is an American lodging. He professes to be a doctor, but does not look like one. In fact, if one judged by his looks, he might be – well, a perfect

ruffian. *No one knows anything about him. He never does any work, and always seems rather hard up, although he pays his rent regularly. He must wear something over his boots that enables him to walk silently, for no one ever hears him come in. At intervals he disappears for a time.'*

Meanwhile, press speculation continued unabated. *The Times* recorded that:

'A somewhat important fact has been pointed out, which puts a fresh complexion on the theory of the murders. It appears that cattle boats bringing in live freight to London are in the habit of coming into the Thames on Thursdays or Fridays, and leave for the continent on Sundays or Mondays. It has already been a matter of comment that the recent revolting crimes have been committed at the week's end, and an opinion has been formed among some of the detectives that the murderer is a drover or butcher employed on one of these boats – of which there are many – and that he periodically appears and disappears with one of the steamers. This theory is held to be of much importance by those engaged in this investigation, who believe that the murderer does not reside either in the locality or even in the country at all. It is thought that he may be either a person employed upon one of these boats or one who is allowed to

travel by them, and inquiries have been directed to follow up the theory. It is pointed out that at the inquests on the previous victims the coroners have expressed the opinion that the knowledge of anatomy possessed by a butcher would have been sufficient to enable him to find and cut out the parts of the body which in several cases were obstructed.'

During October the Ripper was conspicuously absent from the capital and life in the East End began to return to normality, although there was much morbid interest in the discovery of a limbless and headless torso found in a cellar of the new Metropolitan Police Headquarters under construction on the Thames Embankment. The location must have been chosen to taunt the police, but even though the scene of the crime was right under their noses, they were never able to solve it. The Whitehall Mystery, as it became known, was not, however, related to the Whitechapel murders, despite rumours to the contrary.

Some attributed the respite in the Ripper killings to the increased police presence, others to the hope that the Ripper had been identified and secretly committed to an asylum or had sought a new killing ground. But the reprieve proved only temporary. On Thursday 8 November 1888 the Ripper returned to Whitechapel to claim what many believe was his final victim.

Fair as a lily

It is a sad fact that the only occasion on which the Ripper's victims were

*The body of
Mary Kelly –
see also page 80*

photographed was in the mortuary. Women of their class and means would not even have had the price of a wedding photograph. It is particularly poignant in the case of Mary Jane Kelly who, according to her friends, was 'tall and pretty, and as fair as a lily, a very pleasant girl who seemed to be on good terms with everybody' and 'one of the most decent and nicest girls you could meet when she was sober'. Unlike the earlier middle-aged victims she was just 25, with a fresh complexion and a fine head of red hair which cascaded down her back. Mary Kelly was the only victim who had her photograph taken at the murder site and it is one which is still disturbing to look upon a century later.

It was said that she had once beguiled a gentleman who had taken her to live with him in France but that it hadn't worked out and she had returned to London, where she began a volatile relationship with Billingsgate fish market porter Joe Barnett. She and Joe would frequently drink their rent money and be forced to find new lodgings. By autumn 1888 they had found a cramped, squalid, ground-floor room for 4s 6d a week at Miller's Court, off Dorset Street in Spitalfields, which was to be the scene of the most notorious murder in criminal history.

In the late afternoon of 30 October 1888 Mary and Joe had an argument, possibly over her insistence on having another prostitute staying with them, Lizzie Albrook, who may have been her lesbian lover. Or they may simply have fallen out over money as Joe had recently lost his job and Mary resented having to go back on the streets to support him. Whatever the reason, he left and did not return until Thursday 8 November, the evening of her murder, to offer her money and try to patch things up. She was having none of it and ordered him to leave, which he apparently did shortly before 8pm without further incident. Maria Harvey, a friend of Mary's, was a witness to this last meeting and described the pair as parting on the best of terms.

A gruesome killing

Some criminologists have tried to make a case for Joe being her killer, but while it is true that obsessive love can so readily turn to hate, the mutilations inflicted on Mary Kelly are inconsistent with the psychological profile of men who kill their former lovers. Some can't bring themselves to kill the person who rejected them and so turn on a substitute. Others will assuage their anguish with a clean kill – a single fatal blow – and then cover the body or lay it out in peaceful repose in an attempt to atone for, or to deny, their crime. Many will exorcise their rage over rejection by repeated blows or cuts and dispose of the body by fire, dismemberment, submerging it or burial. Nowhere in the history of crime, as far as we know, has a jilted lover or betrayed partner performed a frenzied autopsy on their former beloved and then left their handiwork for all to see, as was done to Mary Kelly. No matter how enraged Barnett might have been (and there is no evidence whatsoever to indicate that he took the break-up badly) he could not have sustained that level of hatred towards his former lover over so many hours and then left her defiled corpse for strangers to stare at.

The body had been mutilated to such an extent that Joe could identify Mary only by the shape of an ear and the colour of her eyes, a detail which has led some Ripperologists to wonder if it was really Mary whose body had been found at the scene. Their scepticism is fuelled by the statement of another witness, Mrs Maxwell, who claimed to have met Mary in the street at 8.30am and an hour later on that Friday morning, but it is almost certain that she was mistaken and that it had been the day before.

Murder in Miller's Court

Friday 9 November was an important date in the capital. It was the day of the Lord Mayor's show, when the Mayor would take the oath of office, and then lead a grand procession through the city. It was a public holiday and Mary was intent on seeing the parade. But first she had to earn her rent for that week or she would be turned out once again. She was 29 shillings in arrears and needed to find a punter or two before the landlord sent his rent collector with threats of eviction.

Refreshment stands in Whitechapel

At approximately 2am that Friday morning Mary propositioned labourer George Hutchinson, but when he refused to go with her or to lend her any money she walked away. Hutchinson claims that she talked to another man, who in all likelihood was her murderer, although it is possible that Hutchinson invented the story to divert suspicion from himself. The newspapers were certainly very sceptical regarding the uncanny accuracy of his memory and his capacity to discern small details in a ill-lit street at such an hour.

A correspondent for the *Graphic* wrote on 17 November 1888:

'Even if the murders of last Christmas week and of August 7th be excluded as not certainly belonging to the same series, there still remain five butcheries, all apparently perpetrated by one and the same individual. Concerning this individual, all that can be positively affirmed is that he possesses the skill, either of a butcher or of a medical man, in the art of cutting up animals, human or otherwise. It is true that on this last occasion a man has given a very precise description of the supposed murderer. The very exactitude of his description, however, engenders a feeling of scepticism. The witness in question admits that at the time he saw him he did not suspect the person he watched of being the Whitechapel assassin; yet, at two o'clock in the morning, in badly-lighted thoroughfares, he observed more than most of us would observe in broad daylight, with ample time at our disposal. A man who in such a hasty survey notes such points as "a pair of dark 'spats,' with light buttons, over button boots," and "a red stone hanging from his watch-chain," must possess the eyes of a born detective. Granting, however, that this description is accurate, and not due to the after-effects of a lively imagination, it is evidence that the clue thus given is an important one, inasmuch as it shows that the murderer belongs to a superior class.'

Hutchinson later gave a statement to the police in which he said that he watched Mary and her companion for some time, which accounted for the degree of detail he was able to recall.

'He then placed his right hand around her shoulders. He also had a kind of a small parcel in his left hand with a kind of strap round it. I stood against the lamp of the Queen's Head Public House and watched him. They both then came past me and the man hung down his head with his hat over his eyes. I stooped down and looked him in the face. He looked at me stern. They both went into Dorset Street. I followed them. They both stood at the corner of the court for about 3 minutes. He said something to her. She said, 'alright my dear come along you will be comfortable'. He then placed his arm on her shoulder and gave her a kiss. She said she had lost her handkerchief. He then pulled his handkerchief, a red

"HE TURNED AND LOOKED AT ME."

Hutchinson witnesses Mary meeting with her murderer

one, out and gave it to her. They both then went up the court together. I then went to the court to see if I could see them but could not. I stood there for about three quarters of an hour to see if they came out. They did not so I went away.'

Hutchinson described the man as 'aged about 34 or 35, height 5 ft. 6, complexion pale, dark eyes and eye lashes, slight moustache curled up each end and hair dark, very surly-looking; dress, long dark coat, collar and cuffs trimmed astrakhan and a dark jacket under, light waistcoat, dark trousers, dark felt hat turned down in the middle, button boots and gaiters with white buttons, black tie with horse shoe pin, respectable appearance, walked very sharp, Jewish appearance.'

He added yet more details at a later date: 'His watch chain had a big seal, with a red stone, hanging from it . . . He had no side whiskers, and his chin was clean shaven . . . I believe that he lives in the neighbourhood, and I fancied that I saw him in Petticoat Lane on Sunday morning, but I was not certain.'

The question remains, however, why Hutchinson felt the need to linger. What was his interest in Mary Kelly? The police clearly accepted his statement at face value as they immediately circulated the description he had given them to all the stations in the city.

Witness reports

Perhaps a more reliable sighting was that made by laundress Sarah Lewis, who saw a man lurking around Miller's Court at 2.30am, half an hour after Hutchinson claimed to have seen Mary with the man who must have been her murderer. It was the same man who had accosted Lewis and a friend a few days earlier. He was short, aged about 40, pale-faced with a black moustache and wore a short black coat and carried a long black bag.

Lewis was disturbed to see him again as he had an unsettling manner and on the previous occasion had insisted that she and her female friend should accompany him. Eventually she and her friend had run off, so frightened were they of what he might do, although nothing explicit had been said and no threats had been made. Their intuition may have saved their lives, whereas Mary Kelly was too drunk to have heeded hers.

Earlier that evening, around 11.45 pm, another prostitute living in Miller's Court, Mary Ann Cox, had observed Mary Kelly in the company of a man and noted that Kelly was so drunk that her speech was slurred. Mrs Cox later gave a description of the man to the police in which she described him as being 'about 36 years old, about 5 ft 6 in high, complexion fresh and I believe he had blotches on his face, small side whiskers, and a thick carroty moustache, dressed in shabby dark clothes, dark overcoat and black felt hat'.

Mrs Cox recalled that Mary had a knitted red crossover covering her shoulders and a dark threadbare linsey frock. As they passed each other in the narrow courtyard Mary told her, 'I am going to have a song.' After Mrs Cox entered her room she heard Mary softly singing 'A Violet I Plucked From Mother's Grave', which she was still singing some time after 1am when Mrs Cox went back out in the drizzling rain. She returned at 3am, by which time there was no sound from Mary's room and the light that had shone through the torn curtains was out. For the next few hours Mrs Cox lay on her bed unable to sleep and listening to the rain. She heard nothing until 5.45am when she heard someone leaving, but from which room she could not say. She thought it may have been a policeman making his round, as it was too late for the residents who worked in the market. In retrospect, she may have heard the last exit of Jack the Ripper.

The discovery of Mary Kelly

Mary Kelly's body was discovered at 10.45am by the rent collector Thomas Bowyer who, having had no answer, had put his hand through a broken window and pushed back the coat which served as a makeshift curtain to peer inside. What he saw that morning haunted him for the rest of his life. When he had recovered himself sufficiently he ran to his employer, landlord John McCarthy, who owned a grocer shop on the corner at 37 Dorset Street.

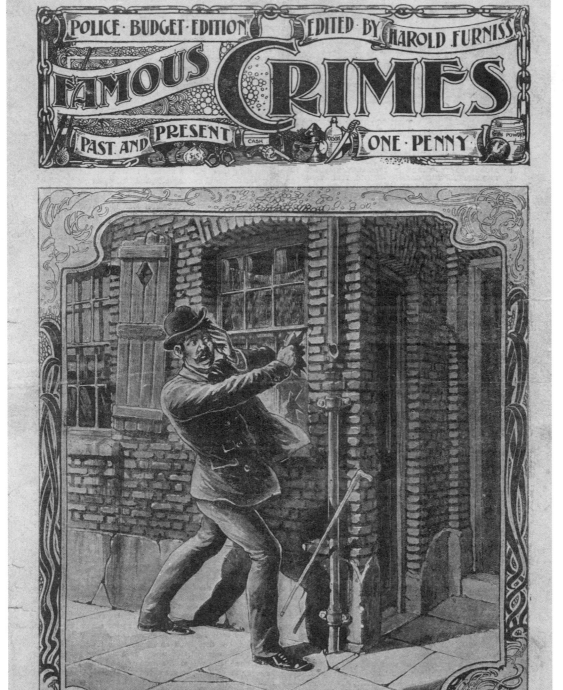

POLICE·BUDGET·EDITION   EDITED BY HAROLD FURNISS

FAMOUS CRIMES

PAST AND PRESENT   ONE·PENNY

THE DISCOVERY OF THE SIXTH "RIPPER" MURDER.

Vol. II.—No. 18.

The Times managed to secure an eye-witness account of the murder scene from McCarthy, who returned to Miller's Court with Inspector Walter Beck and Detective Walter Dew. They broke the door down and were confronted with what Dew later described as a sight he would never forget until his dying day.

McCarthy told reporters, 'The sight I saw was more ghastly even than I had prepared myself for. On the bed lay the body . . . while the table was covered with what seemed to me to be lumps of flesh. The sight we saw I cannot drive away from my mind. It looked more like the work of a devil than of a man. The poor woman's body was lying on the bed, undressed. She had been completely disembowelled, and her entrails had been taken out and placed on the table. It was those that I had seen when I looked through the window and took to be lumps of flesh. The woman's nose had been cut off, and her face gashed beyond recognition. Both her breasts too had been cut clean away and placed by the side of her liver and other entrails on the table. I had heard a great deal about the Whitechapel murders, but I declare to God I had never expected to see such a sight as this. The body was, of course, covered with blood, and so was the bed. The whole scene is more than I can describe. I hope I may never see such a sight again.'

The Times described the murder scene:

'A more horrible or sickening sight could not be imagined. The clothes of the woman were lying by the side of the bed, as though they had been taken off and laid down in the ordinary manner. It was a very poorly furnished apartment, about 12 ft. square, there being only an old bedstead, two old tables and a chair in it. The bedclothes had been turned down, and this was probably done by the murderer after he had cut his victim's throat. There was no appearance of a struggle having taken place, and, although a careful search of the room was made, no knife or instrument of any kind was found . . . at 10 minutes to 4 o'clock a one-horse carrier's cart, with the ordinary tarpaulin cover was driven into Dorset Street, and halted opposite Millerscourt. From the cart was taken a long shell or coffin, dirty and scratched with constant use. This was taken into the death chamber, and there the remains were temporarily coffined. The news that the body was about to be removed caused a great rush of people from the courts running out of Dorset Street, and there was a determined effort to break the police cordon at the Commercial Street end.*

The crowd, which pressed round the van, was of the humblest class, but the demeanour of the poor people was all that could be described. Ragged caps were doffed and slatternly-looking women shed tears as the shell, covered with a ragged-looking cloth, was placed in the van. The remains were taken to the Shoreditch Mortuary, where they will remain until they have been viewed by the coroner's jury.'

The very last sighting of Jack the Ripper?

A curious postscript to the murder at Miller's Court was the sighting of a man near the crime scene that Friday morning who answered the description given by Sarah Lewis. According to *The Times:*

'A Mrs Paumier, a young woman who sells roasted chestnuts at the corner of

The broken window is arrowed in this photograph of Mary Kelly's lodging house taken the day after her murder

Widegate Street, a narrow thoroughfare about two minutes' walk from the scene of the murder, told a reporter yesterday afternoon a story which appears to afford a clue to the murderer. She said that about 12 o'clock that morning a man dressed like a gentleman came up to her and said, "I suppose you have heard about the murder in Dorset Street." She replied that she had, whereupon the man grinned and said, "I know more about it than you." He then stared into her face and went down Sandy's Row, another narrow thoroughfare which cuts across Widegate Street. Whence he had got some way off, however, he vanished. Mrs Paumier said the man had a black moustache, was about 5ft 6in high, and wore a black silk hat, a black coat, and speckled trousers. He also carried a black shiny bag about a foot in depth and a foot and a half in length. Mrs Paumier stated further that the same man accosted three young women, whom she knew, on Thursday night, and they chaffed him and asked him what he had in the bag, and he replied, "Something that the ladies don't like."

One of the three young women she named, Sarah Roney, a girl about 20 years of age, states that she was with two other girls on Thursday night in Brushfield Street which is near Dorset Street, when a man wearing a tall hat and a black coat, and carrying a black bag, came up to her and said, "Will you come with me?" She told him that she would not, and asked him what he had in the bag, and he said, "Something the ladies don't like." He then walked away.'

'**I suppose you have heard about the murder in Dorset Street.' 'I know more about it than you'**

A further report received late last night says:

'Not the slightest doubt appears to be entertained in official headquarters that this fresh crime is by the same hand which committed the others. There is also, it is to be noted, a striking similarity of the month in which the crime has been committed, for while two of the most atrocious of the other murders in the same district were committed on the 7th of the month of September and August, this was committed on the 8th – approximately the same period in the month. This would seem to indicate that the murderer was absent from the scene of these horrors for fixed periods, and that his return was always about the same time. The late storms might account for the crime on this occasion being a day later, the suggestion, of course, being that the murderer journeys across the sea on some of the short passages.'

Profile of a murderer

In his official report to Sir Charles Warren, dated the same day as *The*

Times story, 10 November, Dr Bond, lecturer in forensic medicine at Westminster Hospital, reviewed the particulars of each killing and provided a rudimentary profile of the perpetrator.

'The murderer must have been a man of physical strength & of great coolness & daring there is no evidence that he had an accomplice. He must in my opinion be a man subject to periodical attacks of Homicidal & erotic mania. The character of the mutilations indicate that the man may be in a condition, sexually, that may be called Satyriasis [a condition of being exceedingly oversexed]. It is of course possible that the Homicidal impulse may have developed from a revengeful or brooding condition of the mind, or that religious mania may have been the original disease but I do not think either hypothesis is likely. The murderer in external appearance is quite likely to be a quiet "inoffensive-looking man" probably middle aged & neatly & respectably dressed. I think he must be in the habit of wearing a cloak or overcoat or he could hardly have escaped notice in the streets if the blood on his hands or clothes were visible.

Assuming the murderer to be such a person as I have just described, he would probably be solitary & eccentric in his habits, also he is most likely to be a man without regular occupation, but with some small income or pension. He is possibly living among respectable persons who have some knowledge of his character and habits and who may have grounds for suspicion that he is not quite right in his mind at times. Such persons would probably be unwilling to communicate suspicions to the Police for fear of trouble or notoriety whereas if there were prospect of a reward it might overcome their scruples.'

The seventh victim?

Former Chief Constable Frederick Porter Wensley began his career as a beat constable in the Metropolitan Police in January 1888 and was seconded to H Division, where he was directly involved in the investigation of the Whitechapel murders. The following extract is taken from his memoirs, *Forty Years of Scotland Yard*, published in 1931.

'During my first year of service the Jack the Ripper murders occurred in Whitechapel. Again and again bodies of women, murdered and mutilated, were found in the East End; but every effort to bring the assassin to justice failed. For a while there was an atmosphere of terror in the district.

This business brought about my first glimpse of the neighbourhood in which so much of my life was to be spent. In view of the work that I was to do there later there was a touch of coincidence in the fact that my earliest recollections should be concerned with a great murder mystery.

Not that I had much to do with it. In common with hundreds of others I was

drafted there, and we patrolled the streets – usually in pairs – without any tangible result . . . Officially, only five (with a possible sixth) murders were attributed to Jack the Ripper. There was, however, at least one other, strikingly similar in method, in which the murderer had a very narrow escape. This occurred something more than two years after the supposed last Ripper murder.

The story is chiefly concerned with a very young officer named Ernest Thompson who had been only six weeks in the service when, on February 13, 1891 – an ominous date – he went out for the first time alone on night duty. A part of his beat was through Chambers Street, from which at that time a turning, most inappropriately named Swallow Gardens, ran under a dark, dismal railway arch towards the Royal Mint. Thompson was patrolling Chambers Street when a man came running out of Swallow Gardens towards him. As soon as he perceived the officer he turned tail, made off at speed *in the opposite direction, and was in a few seconds lost to view.*

Thompson moved into Swallow Gardens and on turning the corner came across the body of a murdered woman – Frances Coles – mutilated in much the same fashion as the victims of the Ripper. The spot had possibly been chosen because it commanded a view in three directions.

Victim of the Ripper? Frances Coles

It is probable that had Thompson been a little more experienced he would have taken up the chase of the fugitive immediately. In all likelihood he would have made a capture which might possibly have solved a great mystery. But it is understandable that this young man was so taken aback by his grim discovery that he did not take the obvious steps. It

was certainly through no lack of personal courage, as later events showed.

Whether the murderer was Jack the Ripper or not, he escaped. I fancy that the lost opportunity preyed on Thompson's mind, for I heard him refer to it in despondent terms more than once, and he seemed to regard the incident as presaging some evil fate for himself. By an uncanny coincidence his forebodings came true. The first time he went on night duty he discovered a murder; the last time he went on duty, some years later, he was murdered himself.'

Wensley's account of the Francis Coles killing is inaccurate in one important respect – he describes the 26-year-old prostitute as having been mutilated 'in much the same fashion as the victims of the Ripper', whereas only her throat was slashed. Dr Phillips, the police surgeon who had carried out post-mortems on previous Ripper victims, was adamant that the fatal injuries were not the handiwork of the Ripper. Moreover, the suspect in the Coles killing did not evade the police for long but was later identified as James Sadler, a ship's fireman who was known for his violent temper and who had been seen arguing with Coles on the night of her death. But he was never charged with the killing for lack of evidence.

A year later the official police file on the Whitechapel murders was closed. The 'Autumn of Terror' was at an end.

More possible victims

The following women were extremely unlikely to have been Ripper victims, but it is just possible that one or more may have provided a rehearsal for his escalating cycle of violence.

Fairy Fay was the appellation given by the *Daily Telegraph* to an unnamed murder victim reputedly found on 26 December 1887 who was allegedly killed by having 'a stake thrust through her abdomen'. However, no such person appears in any police files or in the records of the local authority. It seems likely that Fairy Fay may have been a 'Jane Doe' type tag used by a journalist to denote Emma Smith, who had been fatally injured in a similar way. *The Telegraph* was clearly referring to the Emma Smith attack, but was mistaken about the date.

Annie Millwood, aged approximately 38, was subjected to a vicious attack and hospitalized on 25 February 1888 for the 'numerous stabs in the legs and lower part of the body' which hastened her death a month later.

Ada Wilson was stabbed twice in the neck on 28 March 1888 and survived.

Emma Elizabeth Smith was attacked by three men, probably extortionists, on 3 April 1888, and a blunt object was inserted into her vagina. She died in hospital two days later. Her death is included because it is commonly cited by many Ripper scholars as the first Ripper murder, although the victim's own statement shows that to be a false assumption.

Annie Farmer claimed to have been the victim of a knife attack on 21 November 18881, but the injury was superficial which led police to believe that it may have been self-inflicted to bring attention to herself. Consequently no further investigation was deemed necessary.

Rose Mylett (also known as Catherine Millett and Alice Downey) was strangled on 20 December 1888, possibly accidentally after becoming entangled in a cord while drunk.

Elizabeth Jackson was dismembered and the parts tossed into the Thames in the summer of 1889. Although she was a prostitute it is more likely that she was the victim of the 'torso' murderer who had deposited an earlier victim in the cellar of the new Metropolitan Police headquarters the previous year.

Alice McKenzie (alias Alice Bryant) had her throat slashed on 17 July 1889 and was left to bleed to death. The cause of death reawakened fears that the Ripper may have returned but her other injuries suggested a domestic quarrel that had got out of hand.

The Pinchin Street Murder The name given to the third 'torso murder' victim discovered on 10 September 1889 who was later identified as prostitute Lydia Hart. It is feasible that the torso murderer and Jack the Ripper were one and the same, but there is no conclusive evidence to connect both sets of killings.

Questions in the Commons

On 9 November Sir Charles Warren resigned as head of the Metropolitan Police in response to increasing personal criticism of his handling of the case and specifically for ordering the erasure of the Goulston Street graffiti which may have offered a vital clue to the Ripper's identity.

As a consequence of Warren's departure the Home Secretary, Henry Matthews, was pressed to account for the failure of the police in apprehending the murderer. During questions in the House of Commons Matthews countered by stating:

'The failure, so far, to detect the persons guilty of the Whitechapel murders is due, not to any new organization, or to any defect in the existing system, but to the extraordinary cunning and secrecy which characterize these atrocious crimes. I have already, for some time, had under consideration the whole system of the Criminal Investigation Department, with a view to introducing any improvement, that experience may suggest. With regard to the final question of the hon. member for Camborne, I have to say that Sir Charles Warren did, on the 8th inst., tender his resignation to Her Majesty's Government, and that it has been accepted.' (Loud Opposition cheers.)

On a subsequent occasion the Home Secretary was asked whether he contemplated offering any additional reward for the capture of the Whitechapel murderer. His response revealed the degree to which the government feared the threat of civil unrest should the police fail to apprehend the murderer in their midst.

'I hope the House will allow me, at greater length than is usual in answering a question, to state why I have refrained from offering a reward in the Whitechapel cases. Before 1884 it was the frequent practice of the Home Office to offer rewards, sometimes of large amount, in serious cases. In 1883, in particular, several rewards, ranging from £200 to £2,000, were offered in such cases as the murder of Police-constable Boans and the dynamite explosions in Charles-Street and at various railway stations. These rewards, like the reward of £10,000 in the Phoenix Park murders proved ineffectual, and produced no evidence of any value . . . Since I have been at the Home Office I have followed the rule thus deliberately laid down and steadily adhered to by my predecessors. I do not mean that the rule may not be subject to exceptions, as, for instance, where it is known who the criminal is, and information is wanted only as to his hiding place, or on account of other circumstances of the crime itself. In the Whitechapel murders, not only are these conditions wanting at present, but the danger of a false charge is intensified by the excited state of public feeling. I know how desirable it is to allay that public feeling, and I should have been glad if

13. The Ripper not only hastened Warren's resignation as police chief, but nearly unseated Home Secretary Henry Matthews, who was accused of 'philandering with pothouse Tories while God's poor are being slaughtered wholesale in London'. Even Lord Salisbury, the Prime Minister, did not escape criticism.

*the circumstances had justified me in giving visible proof that the authorities are not heedless or indifferent. I beg to assure the honourable member and the House that neither the Home Office nor Scotland Yard will leave a stone unturned in order to bring to justice the perpetrator of these abominable crimes, which have outraged the feelings of the entire community.
(Hear, hear.)'*

An opposition MP then asked whether the Home Secretary had 'taken into consideration the propriety of extending the offer of pardon to an accomplice to the murders, having regard to the fact that in the case of the first murder committed last Christmas, according to the dying woman [Emma Smith], several persons were concerned in the murder.'

Mr Mathews said it would not be proper that he would consider the suggestion. On 18 July the Secretary of State was again pressed on the question of whether he would offer a substantial reward, 'accompanied by a free pardon, to anyone not in the police force and not the actual perpetrator of the recent crime in Whitechapel who would give such information as would lead to the conviction of the murderer; and whether he would sufficiently increase the number of detectives so as to prevent, if possible, further atrocities in East London.' His answer was intended to put an end to the matter.

'I have consulted the Commissioner of Police, and he informs me that he has no reason to believe that the offer of a reward now would be productive of any good result, and he does not recommend any departure from the policy resolved on last year, and fully explained by me to the House. Since the occurrence of the outrages in the East-end a large number of men in plain clothes have been employed there, and I yesterday sanctioned an arrangement for still further increasing the number of detectives available for duty in Whitechapel.'

An autumn evening in Whitechapel

On 3 November 1888, *Littell's Living Age*, an American magazine, printed the following graphic description of life in the East End during the 'Autumn of Terror':

'Whitechapel and Spitalfields are always interesting neighbourhoods, and recent events have made them decidedly more interesting. They have afforded startling illustrations of the dreadful possibilities of life down in the unfathomable depths of these vast human warrens. At all times one who strolls through this quarter of town, especially by night, must feel that below his ken are the awful deeps of an ocean teeming with life, but enshrouded in impenetrable mystery. As he catches here and there a glimpse of a face under the flickering, uncertain light of a lamp –

the face perhaps of some woman, bloated by drink and distorted by passion – he may get a momentary shuddering sense of what humanity may sink to when life is lived apart from the sweet, health-giving influences of fields and flowers, of art and music and books and travel, of the stimulus of interesting enterprise, the gentle amenities of happy hours and intercourse with the educated and the cultured. A momentary sense of what human nature may become may here and there flash in upon one as he gazes out upon the dark waters, but it is only when the human monster actually rises for a moment to the surface and disappears again, leaving a victim dead and disembowelled, that one quite realizes that that momentary scene is a dread reality. Just for a few days the mass of the people of Spitalfields and Whitechapel themselves seemed to be realizing the awful possibilities of the nature that belonged to them. Thousands of them were really shocked and sobered, by the last tragedy especially. One could see in the people's faces, and could detect in their tones and answers, an indefinable something which told plainly that they had been horrified by a revelation.

The street is oppressively dark, though at present the gloom is relieved somewhat by feebly lighted shopfronts. Men are lounging at the doors of the shops, smoking evil-smelling pipes. Women with bare heads and with arms under their aprons are sauntering about in twos and threes, or are seated

'The Cimmerian darkness of lower London indoors and out constitutes no small part of its wretchedness...'

gossiping on steps leading into passages dark as Erebus. Now round the corner into another still gloomier passage, for there are no shops here to speak of. This is the notorious Wentworth Street. The police used to make a point of going through this only in couples, and possibly may do so still when they go there at all. Just now there are none met with. It is getting on into the night, but gutters, and doorways, and passages, and staircases appear to be teeming with children. See there in that doorway of a house without a glimmer of light about it. It looks to be a baby in long clothes laid on the floor of the passage, and seemingly exhausted with crying. Listen for a moment at this next house. There is a scuffle going on upon the staircase – all in the densest darkness – and before you have passed a dozen yards there is a rush down-stairs and an outsurging into the street with fighting and screaming, and an outpouring of such horrible blackguardism that it makes you shudder as you look at those curly-headed preternaturally sharp-witted children who leave their play to gather around the mêlée. God help the little mortals! How can they become anything but savages, "pests of society," the "dangerous classes," and so on? How black and unutterably gloomy all the houses look! How infinitely all the moral and physical wretchedness of such localities as these is intensified by the darkness of the streets and the houses. It is wise and astute of Mr. Barnett to give emphatic expression to the cry that has so often been raised for "more light" for lower London. If in this one matter of light alone, the streets and houses of the West End were reduced to the condition of the East, what would life become there? Oh, for a great installation of the electric light, with which, as the sun goes down, to deluge the streets and lanes, the dark alleys and passages, the staircases and rooms of this nether world. Homes would become cleaner, and more cheerful and attractive; life would become healthier, whole masses of crime would die out like toadstools under sunlight, and what remained would be more easily dealt with. The Cimmerian darkness of lower London indoors and out constitutes no small part of its wretchedness, and the brilliant lighting of the public-house gives it much of its attraction. Even the repute of many of these shady localities is due in great measure to their impenetrable gloom after nightfall.

It is a relief to get out of this vile little slum and to work one's way back into the life and light of the great highway, with its flaunting shops, its piles of glowing fruit, its glittering jewellery, its steaming cook-shops, its flaring gin-palaces and noisy shows, and clubs and assembly rooms, and churches and mission halls, its cheap jacks and shooting galleries, its streaming naphtha lights and roar and rattle, and hurrying throngs and noisy groups, and little assemblies gathered together under the stars and the street-lamps to listen to some expounder of the mysteries of the *universe or of the peculiar merits of a new patent pill. Here are the newspaper contents-bill spread out at large with some of the newsvendor's own additions and amplifications, telling of new murders or further details of the old ones. The young man with a bundle of papers under his arm is evidently on the friendliest of terms with the neighboring shoeblack. One or the other of them has picked up half a cigar, and the two are getting alternate pulls at it with evident enjoyment. Up in a retired corner there is a little mob gathered round an almost inanimate-looking figure beating out with a couple of quills what he takes apparently to be music from a sort of home-made dulcimer. A few yards farther on, a boy without any legs is the object of attention; and next comes a group thronging curiously round a four-wheel cab. Nothing can be seen, but as the vehicle drives off towards the hospital and the mob disperses it is generally understood that "she has been knocked about." The only question about which there seems to be any uncertainty is as to whether she is nearly dead or only very drunk.*

A few yards further on there is a waxwork show with some horrible pictorial representations of the recent murders, and all the dreadful details are being blared out into the night, and women with children in their arms are pushing their way to the front with their pennies to see the ghastly objects within. Next door is a show, in which ghosts and devils and skeletons appear to be the

chief attractions; and near at hand is a flaring picture of a modern Hercules performing within.

Out again into the great thoroughfare, back a little way past the roaring salesman and the hideous waxwork, and round the corner. This opening here, where the public-house, the bar of which looks to be full of mothers with children in their arms, blazes at the corner, leads down to Bucks Row. Nobody about here seems at all conscious of the recent tragedy, the only suggestion of which is a bill in the public-house window, offering, on behalf of an enterprising newspaper, a reward of a hundred pounds for the conviction of the criminal. A little way down out of the public-house glare, and Bucks Row looks to be a singularly desolate, out-of-the-way region. But there is a piano-organ grinding out the "Men of Harlech" over the spot where the murdered woman was found; women and girls are freely coming and going through the darkness, and the rattle of sewing-machines, and the rushing of railway trains, and the noisy horseplay of a gang of boys, all seem to be combining with the organ-grinder to drown recollection and to banish all unpleasant reflection. "There seems to be little apprehension of further mischief by this assassin at large," was an observation addressed to a respectable-looking elderly man within a few yards of the house in Hanbury Street, where the latest victim was found. "No; very little. People, most of 'em, think he's gone to Gateshead," was the reply.'

City under pressure: London's population surged in the 19th century from a million in 1800 to six million by 1900

CHAPTER 3 | FORENSIC FILES

The myth of Jack the Ripper came into existence on the morning of 27 September 1888. Prior to that date the deaths of Martha Tabram, Polly Nichols and the earlier, unrelated slaying of Emma Smith had all been attributed to an anonymous fiend known only as the Whitechapel Murderer. But as soon as T.J. Bulling, the editor of the Central News Agency (a clearing house for correspondents) opened a letter addressed to 'The Boss' written in red ink he knew that the British press had a name that would capture the public imagination and sell newspapers in unprecedented numbers.

'Dear Boss,
I keep on hearing the police have caught me but they won't fix me just yet. I have laughed when they look so clever and talk about being on the right track. That joke about Leather Apron gave me real fits. I am down on whores and I shan't quit ripping them till I do get buckled. Grand work the last job was. I gave the lady no time to squeal. How can they catch me now? I love my work and want to start again. You will soon hear of me with my funny little games. I saved some proper red stuff in a ginger beer bottle over the last job to write with but it went thick like glue and I cant use it. Red ink is fit enough I hope. ha ha The next job I do I shall clip the lady's ears off and send to the Police officers just for jolly, wouldn't you? Keep this letter back till I do a bit more work, then give it out straight. My knife's so nice and sharp, I want to get to work right away if I get a chance.
Good luck.
Yours truly
Jack the Ripper
Don't mind me giving the trade name'

·25. Sept.· 1888.

Dear Boss.

I keep on hearing the police have caught me but they wont fix me just yet. I have laughed when they look so clever and talk about being on the right track. That joke about Leather apron gave me real fits. I am down on whores and I shant quit ripping them till I do get buckled. Grand work the last job was. I gave the lady no time to squeal. How can they catch me now. I love my work and want to st again. You will soon hear of me with my funny little games. I saved some of the proper red stuff in a ginger beer bottle over the last job to write with but it went thick like glue and I cant use it. Red ink is fit enough I hope ha. ha. The next job I do I shall clip the ladys ears off and send to the

Genuine message from the Ripper or a waste of police time? Most experts doubt the authenticity of this correspondence

The following was written vertically as a postscript:

'Wasn't good enough to post this before I got all the red ink off my hands curse it. No luck yet. They say I'm a doctor now ha ha'

The choice of name suggested that its creator was an educated man who hid his intelligence behind contrived grammatical errors. The inspiration for the appellation was obvious. The newspapers had been describing the murderer as ripping the bodies while Jack was a traditional name for the more colourful characters of English fiction. Jolly Jack Tar was a generic name for all sailors, the public hangman was traditionally referred to as Jack Ketch, a mischievous rogue would be called Jack the Lad and there were numerous villains synonymous with daring exploits who thumbed their noses at authority such as Spring-heeled Jack and Jack Shepherd the highwayman, who repeatedly escaped from Newgate prison. Clearly its creator was intent on giving the murderer a more romantic image. Only an irresponsible journalist would have no reservations about re-inventing a depraved serial killer as a daring rascal. The murderer is more likely to have viewed his bloody spree in vainglorious terms, perhaps as a holy crusade to rid the world of disease-riddled 'undesirables'. He would have been insulted to think that the more popular press viewed him as a music-hall villain.

A second letter

On the Monday morning following the murders of Elizabeth Stride and Catherine Eddowes the Central News Agency received a second letter in the same handwriting postmarked October 1:

'I wasn't codding dear old Boss when I gave you the tip. youll hear about saucy Jack's work tomorrow double event this time. Number one squealed a bit couldn't finish straight off. Had no time to get ears for police thanks for keeping last letter back till I got to work again.
Jack the Ripper'

Knowing that they would not be able to prevent the letters from being published, Scotland Yard circulated copies to every police station with instructions that they should be put on display in the hope that someone might recognize the handwriting. The result was a flood of crank correspondence from all over the world by unstable individuals and malicious hoaxers who thought it would be fun to taunt the police.

One of the factors that casts doubt upon the authenticity of the first two letters is the fact that the writer did not send the victim's ears to the police as he promised even though he had sufficient time to do so. Furthermore, the second letter did not predict the double murder committed on Sunday 30 September as is commonly thought. The letter was apparently posted on either Sunday night or Monday morning when the whole district would have been electrified with news of the killings at Berner Street and Mitre Square.

Modern London police officers John Douglas and Mark Olshaker dismiss the letters out of hand, as did their predecessor Sir Charles Warren. 'It's too organized, too indicative of intelligence and rational thought, and far too "cutesy",' declare Douglas and Olshaker. 'An offender of this type would never think of his actions as "funny little games" or say that his "knife's so nice and sharp".'

The third taunt

A third communication was received by the Central News Agency on 5 October.

'Dear Friend,
In the name of God hear me I swear I did not kill the female whose body was found at Whitchall. If she was an honest woman I will hunt down and destroy her murderer. If she was a whore God will bless the hand that slew her, for the women of Moab and Midian shall die and their blood shall mingle with the dust. I never harm any others or the Divine power that protects and helps me

No return address: letter from the Ripper?

in my grand work would quit for ever.

Do as I do and the light of glory shall shine upon you. I must get to work tomorrow treble event this time yes yes three must be ripped. will send you a bit of face by post I promise this dear old Boss. The police now reckon my work a practical joke well well Jacky's a very practical joker ha ha ha Keep this back till three are wiped out and you can show the cold meat

Yours truly
Jack the Ripper

Despite the boast there was no triple murder, which suggests that the author was not the killer – but if he was not, then why make the boast?

It is very likely that the agency's own journalists were responsible for writing the three 'Dear Boss' letters, probably Bulling and his boss Charles Moore, who were suspected by Scotland Yard of having perpetrated the hoax in order to keep the story simmering and the newspaper proprietors eager to retain their agency's services. If so, they can be credited with creating one of the most enduring trade names in history, but also with having wasted considerable police resources which were diverted from the investigation in the mistaken belief that this was a genuine communication from the murderer. Both men were shrewd enough to realize that a killer attracts little public interest until the press attach a sinister soubriquet to capture the imagination – a strategy which is

as true today as it was 100 years ago.

Sir Robert Anderson was in no doubt that the letters were a hoax and even accuses an employee of the agency in his memoirs:

'The Jack the Ripper letter which is preserved in the Police Museum at New Scotland Yard is the creation of an enterprising London journalist.'

Sir Melville Macnaghten came to the same conclusion:

'In this ghastly production I have always thought I could discern the stained forefinger of the journalist, indeed, a year later, I had shrewd suspicions as to the actual author! But whoever did pen the gruesome stuff, it is certain to my mind that it was not the mad miscreant who had committed the murders. The name "Jack the Ripper", however, had got abroad in the land and had "caught on"; it riveted the attention of the classes as well as the masses.'

Macnaghten's suspicion appears to be borne out by crime writer R. Thurston Hopkins, who in 1935 wrote:

'It was perhaps a fortunate thing that the handwriting of this famous letter was perhaps not identified, for it would have led to the arrest of a harmless Fleet Street journalist. This poor fellow had a breakdown and became a whimsical figure in Fleet Street, only befriended by staff of newspapers and printing works.

He would creep about the dark courts waving his hands furiously in the air, would utter stentorian "Ha ha ha's," and then, meeting some pal, would buttonhole him and pour into his ear all the "inner story" of the East End murders. Many old Fleet Streeters had very shrewd suspicions that this irresponsible fellow wrote the famous Jack the Ripper letter, and even Sir Melville L. Macnaghten, Chief of the Criminal Investigation Department, had his eye on him.'

It was sent in a small box with what the sender claimed was a section of Catherine Eddowes' kidney

Of all the police officials involved in the case only Chief Inspector John George Littlechild was brave enough to name the journalist the Yard thought responsible for the 'Dear Boss' letters, but this may have been because Macnaghten and the others were reluctant to risk being sued for libel by accusing the journalists in print, whereas Littlechild named them in a private letter to journalist George Sims.

'With regard to the term "Jack the Ripper" it was generally believed at the Yard that Tom Bullen [Bulling] of the Central News was the originator, but it is probable Moore, who was his chief, was the inventor. It was a smart piece of journalistic work. No journalist of my time got such privileges from Scotland Yard as Bullen. Mr James Munro when Assistant Commissioner, and afterwards Commissioner, relied on his integrity.'

From Hell

So the mystery of the 'Dear Boss' letters appears to have been resolved. However, there was a fourth piece of correspondence which could possibly have been sent by the killer. In contrast to the ornate copperplate script used in the first two letters the fourth is an almost illegible scrawl which is far more suggestive of a deranged mind. Unlike the first three, it was not signed Jack the Ripper. It was sent on 16 October to George Lusk, the head of the Mile End Vigilance Committee, in a small box with what the sender claimed was a section of Catherine Eddowes' kidney. Dr Thomas Openshaw of the London Hospital established that it was a human adult kidney and Dr Brown the police surgeon stated that it exhibited signs of Bright's Disease from which Eddowes was known to have suffered. It was also reported that the kidney had 5cm (2in) of renal artery attached which matched the 2.5cm (1in) that remained in the corpse. Significantly, the organ had been preserved in spirits rather than in the formalin that hospitals used for specimens, making it unlikely that it was a hoax perpetrated by medical students.

The text of the accompanying letter made disturbing reading:

From hell
M Lusk Sor
I send you half the Kidne I took from one women prasarved it for you, tother piece I fried and ate it was ver nise I may send you the bloody knif that took it out if you only wate a whil longer,
   Signed
   Catch me whenYou can
   Mishter Lusk

However, a recently rediscovered contemporary interview with City Police surgeon Dr Brown contradicts the accepted view that the kidney belonged to Eddowes.

'There is no portion of the renal artery adhering to it, it having been trimmed up, so consequently, there could be no correspondence established between the portion of the body from which it was cut. As it exhibits no trace of decomposition, when we consider the length of time that has elapsed since the commission of the murder, we come to the conclusion that the probability is slight of its being a portion of the murdered woman of Mitre Square.'

Fingerprint evidence

At the time of the Whitechapel murders forensic science was still in its infancy. The radical new theory suggesting that criminals could be identified by their unique individual fingerprints was beginning to be acknowledged grudgingly but had still to be proven in a British court of law. As early as 1879 Scottish physician Henry Foulds had used fingerprint evidence to catch a criminal and had drawn the authorities' attention to its potential in an article published in a national magazine. The article sparked a heated public debate as to who was the true discoverer of fingerprinting, Foulds or his rival William Herschel, so the British police had no excuse for claiming that they were unaware of its value. But no one in authority appears to have even considered testing the technique on the 'Dear Boss' letters, for example, or the personal items found at the feet of Annie Chapman.

Although the first forensic laboratory was not established until 1910 it would not have been unrealistic for the London police of the 1880s to have retained hairs from the victim's clothes for comparison with samples taken from each suspect and to have preserved these for future reference whenever a new suspect was brought in for questioning. A single bloody hair had been sufficient to convict a French duke of murdering his wife in 1847, but it took the British authorities another 50 years to appreciate the value of trace evidence.

Even photography, with which Mathew Brady had recorded the carnage on the battlefields of the American Civil War 25 years before the Ripper killings, was a novelty in British crime detection. No photographs were

William Herschel was one of the pioneers of fingerprinting, a technique the police failed to explore in the hunt for the Ripper

taken of any of the murder sites with the exception of the last, Miller's Court, and the only body to be photographed *in situ* was again the last, that of Mary Kelly. The other victims were all photographed after they had been laid out in the mortuary, at which point the prints were of little use other than for identification. Had the Goulston Street graffiti been photographed before Sir Charles Warren had ordered it to be erased, the police might have possessed a vital clue as to its author and therefore its significance.

Again with the exception of Miller's Court, the authorities failed to preserve the crime scenes. After an initial cursory glance around the immediate vicinity of the murders for cart tracks and a murder weapon they allowed crowds of curious onlookers to within a few feet of the bodies, thereby compromising the location and risking the obliteration of vital evidence such as footprints. Any physical clues left at the scene were washed away in the haste to scrub the stains from the streets.

Wasted opportunities

While a handful of resourceful investigators, such as the French criminologist Professor R.A. Reiss, were applying simple scientific methods and deductive reasoning in the manner of Sir Arthur Conan Doyle's infallible fictional detective Sherlock Holmes, the British police still believed that the only sure way of securing a conviction was to catch the culprit in the act, or rely on witnesses and informers to identify the guilty party. Failing that, the alternative was to question everyone in the area at the time of the crime and follow up every lead – and while this method may have been practical for tracking down a known local character who had been seen fleeing the scene of the crime it proved impractical in tracking a shadow. No one had witnessed the Ripper in the act so they couldn't lead the police to him or his associates.

Moreover, the Ripper was not the type of criminal the British police were used to dealing with. He was a lone killer who murdered strangers at random and so there was nothing to tie him to his victims. Had the motive been robbery there was a good chance that the stolen goods might have been traced and the culprit brought to justice. If it had been a crime of passion a relationship might have been established and friends of the deceased might have been pressed to provide a description. But the victims were strangers and the motive appears to have been gratuitous sadism, so instead of pursuing a trail the police scattered in all directions following a thousand false leads down as many blind alleys. With no serious leads to pursue they were forced to investigate suspicions, prejudices and malicious rumours.

The detectives were certainly familiar with the neighbourhood and its criminal fraternity, but they were fatally inflexible and blinkered in their approach to an investigation that demanded a radical new strategy.

Though criminal profiling was not fully developed as an aspect of forensic science until the 1970s, Dr Bond, the police surgeon, offered a detailed sketch of the Ripper in a report to Sir Charles Warren after the final murder (see page 84) in which he implies that the Whitechapel murderer was the Victorian detective's nightmare – a lone unpredictable killer without friends or associates in the criminal underworld who could be induced to inform on him. Like so many serial killers he may have disarmed his victims by assuming an air of vulnerability, or he may have lured them with his superficial charm. By day he probably appeared unremarkable, even harmless, and so would not have drawn suspicion by his actions or his manner. The only people who would have seen the madness in his eyes were his victims in the seconds before he choked the life out of them.

The one thing that can be said of the Ripper killings is that they impressed upon the authorities the obvious need to establish basic crime-scene procedures, specifically the preservation of trace evidence as well as the routine photographing of the crime scenes. It was only with the Ripper killings that the British police were forced to face the fact that their leisurely methods may have been sufficient to catch petty thieves and drunken ruffians, but

they were grossly inadequate for ensnaring an unpredictable, predatory serial killer.

Ten years before the East End atrocities Scotland Yard had established the first plain-clothes detective force, the CID (Criminal Investigation Department) but had failed to arm this elite squad with the modern tools and techniques of crime detection which were readily available. Instead, the British police chose to rely on tried and tested methods which belonged to an earlier age. Jack the Ripper woke them up to the harsh realities of the coming century.

The callous ritual sacrifice of Mary Kelly

It was generally believed at the time of the murders that the Ripper was a religious maniac. If true, it might explain why he mutilated Mary Kelly to the extent that he did and why he ceased his reign of terror immediately afterwards.

Mark Daniel, author of a novelization of the *Jack the Ripper* TV mini-series starring Michael Caine, recently proposed a scenario in which the killing served as a ritual sacrifice made in order to atone for the murderer's previous transgressions and he has identified a specific extract from the Old Testament which may have provided the inspiration.

The presence of an uncommonly large fire in the grate at Miller's Court had puzzled the police at the time as

POLICE NOTICE.

TO THE OCCUPIER.

On the mornings of Friday, 31st August, Saturday 8th, and Sunday, 30th September, 1888, Women were murdered in or near Whitechapel, supposed by some one residing in the immediate neighbourhood. Should you know of any person to whom suspicion is attached, you are earnestly requested to communicate at once with the nearest Police Station.

Metropolitan Police Office,
30th September, 1888.

Printed by McCorquodale & Co. Limited, " The Armoury," Southwark.

it was clearly too big to have been lit solely to provide illumination in such a tiny room. When scraps of clothing were found among the ashes it was presumed that the murderer had used it to consume some of his own blood-stained clothing, but a friend of Kelly's later identified the charred remnants as belonging to clothes she had left earlier that day for Mary to mend. Burnt clothing produces smoke which would have filled the cramped room and made it impossible for the killer to breathe, but human fat would have fed the flames and prevented the fabric from creating smoke.

Chapters 5–7 of Leviticus might provide a clue to the motive behind the murder:

'And if a soul sin . . . then he shall bear his iniquity,
Or if a soul touch any unclean thing . . .
he shall also be unclean, and guilty . . .
Or if he touch the uncleanness of man . . . then he shall be guilty.'

The language may be archaic but the meaning is clear. Sex with a whore, another man or an animal or the touching of unclean meat (as a horse butcher or slaughterman would be forced to do on a daily basis) would be considered a sin against God. Such a sin could only be expunged by a ritual sacrifice.

'And he shall bring his trespass offering unto the Lord for his sin which he hath sinned, a female from the flock . . . for a sin offering . . .
And he shall bring them unto the priest, who shall offer that which is for the sin offering first, and wring off his head from his neck, but shall not divide it asunder . . . And he shall offer the second for a burnt offering . . . and it shall be forgiven him.'

Further verses give instructions for preparing the offering and evoke images of the hideous mutilations uncovered at Miller's Court and the other murder sites.

'It is the burnt offering, because of the burning upon the altar all night unto the morning . . .
And he shall offer of it all the fat thereof, the rump and the fat that covereth the inwards.
And the two kidneys, and the fat which is on them, which is by the flanks, and the caul that is above the liver, with the kidneys, it shall he take away:
. . . And the priest that offereth any man's burnt offering, even the priest shall have to himself the skin of the burnt offering which he hath offered . . .
His own hand shall bring the offerings of the Lord made by fire, the fat with the

breast, it shall he bring . . .
And the right shoulder shall ye give unto the priest for an heave offering . . . '

This scenario might also explain the significance of the Goulston Street graffiti, assuming, of course, that the author was the murderer. 'The Juwes are the men that will not be blamed for nothing' could then be seen as an attempt to blame the Jews for having suggested that one's sins could be forgiven by a ritual killing, a practice foreign to the Christian tradition. By taking instructions from the Bible the Ripper would be able to justify his actions in his own twisted mind and return to some semblance of normal life free of guilt and maybe even with a sense of satisfaction and pride in his work.

The diary of Jack the Ripper?

'Before I have finished all England will know the name I have given myself.'

In 1991 workmen who were carrying out some rewiring in an old Victorian house in Liverpool pulled up the floorboards and found a black leatherbound volume which had lain there undisturbed for more than a century. Many pages had been torn out from the front section leaving just 63 leaves of handwritten entries in a fluid scrawl. But on closer examination it was seen to be no ordinary journal but the psychotic ramblings of a

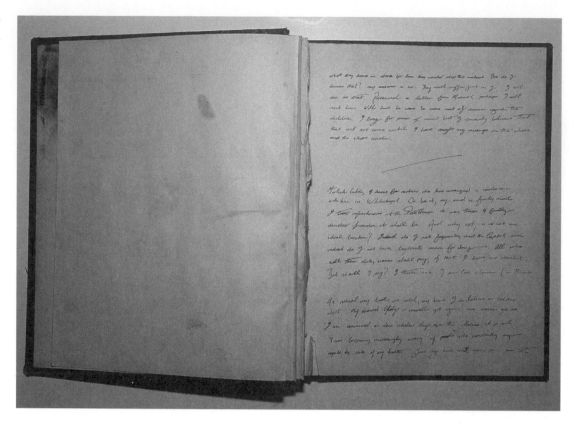

tormented soul who signed the final entry 'Jack the Ripper'.

At least that is the version of events according to a local newspaper. The owner of the diary, scrap metal dealer Michael Barrett, claimed to have been given it by a dying friend, Tony Deveraux, who, we are to assume, obtained it from the workmen who discovered it. Before and after publication, serious doubts were raised as to the diary's authenticity and Barrett was accused of perpetrating a hoax to rival that attempted by the forger of the notorious Hitler diaries, or at least attempting to pass off a forgery by an unidentified source as the genuine article. In his defence Barrett claimed that he pressed his friend to reveal how he came to possess the book, but

Deveraux refused to say anything more. However, Deveraux's daughter denied any knowledge of her father having owned such a book and added that he would have bequeathed it to her had it been his. The new owner of Battlecrease, the house in which it was allegedly found, also denied any knowledge of the discovery, as did the owner of the building firm which carried out the rewiring, who went so far as to question all of his workers. There was, however, a possible if tenuous link, and that is that the building workers were known to drink in the same pub in Liverpool, The Saddle Inn, which Deveraux and Barrett also frequented.

But what would be the significance of the missing pages? Critics of the diary suggested that they were torn out because they would have revealed the identity of the book's real owner and they point out that certain stains and marks prove that it had been a photo album. In response, advocates of the diaries' authenticity argued that the author would have torn out the preceding pages to obliterate any reminder of his wife and family. And they ask why a mentally disturbed individual would purchase a new journal when a defaced family journal would serve a more symbolic, ritualistic purpose.

The author of the diary

As for the 'author' of the disputed diary, we are asked to believe that it was none other than James Maybrick, a wealthy Liverpudlian cotton merchant and the previous owner of Battlecrease, who was poisoned by his wife Florence in May 1889. His murder led to one of the most celebrated trials of the 19th century, but he had never even been considered as a suspect in the Whitechapel murders. The diary does not identify Maybrick by name, but it was allegedly found in a part of the house that had been his study and there are implicit references to his wife and children as well as his wife's lover, against whom he becomes increasingly bitter: 'I long for peace of mind, but I sincerely believe that it will not come until I have sought my revenge on the whore and the whore master.'

This shifting focus from his unfaithful wife to adulterous women in general sounds like the authentic voice of a psychotic, according to forensic psychologist Dr David Forshaw.

But a major problem remains. What connection did a Liverpool businessman have with London's East End? The answer may lie in the following passage.

'Foolish bitch. I know for certain that she has arranged a rendezvous with him in Whitechapel [referring to Whitechapel, Liverpool]. So be it. My mind is finally made. London it shall be and why not? Is it not an ideal location. Whitechapel, Liverpool, Whitechapel, London, ha ha no one could possibly place it together.'

The connection may not be as unlikely as it first appears. In his younger years Maybrick had lived in London's East End and at the time of the murders it is believed that he kept a mistress there. The journey would have been a matter of just a few hours by train, but even so he wouldn't have wanted to undertake it too often and this might account for the long gaps between the killings.

Today it is generally accepted that Polly Nichols was the first Ripper victim, but at the time the deaths of Emma Smith and Martha Tabram were attributed to the Whitechapel murderer, making Nichols the third. As the diary refers to the Bucks Row murder as the first it made it either a contemporary account by the only

Possible suspect: James Maybrick, a wealthy cotton merchant, who had an addiction to strychnine and arsenic

person who knew the truth or a modern fake.

The diary also mentions two small but significant details in the murder of Elizabeth Stride which only the most ardent Ripperologist would know, that she had red hair and that there is a possibility that her throat had been slashed with her own knife.

There is also a reference to two objects found at one of the murder scenes – an empty tin matchbox and a red leather cigarette case which the author of the diary claims to have left behind as a clue. Neither of these two objects were public knowledge until 1987 when the inventory detailing the victim's belongings was published.

Another factor in the diary's favour was the choice of subject. If it was a fake it would have been far easier to have made a lesser suspect fit the facts than Maybrick, whose life is known in greater detail.

A possible suspect?

As for Maybrick having motive, means and opportunity, it is a matter of historical record that his wife had a lover and that Maybrick had an addiction to strychnine and arsenic which, when taken in small doses, were a mild aphrodisiac and stimulant. A habitual user might have delusions of infallibility and be oblivious to danger or the possibility of being caught. Add to this the fact that Maybrick's whereabouts cannot be accounted for on the night of the five 'official'

Whitechapel murders and perhaps there is a compelling case for adding him to the list of suspects.

Maybrick was a well-known hypochondriac and visited his physician an astonishing 70 times during 1888, all of which are a matter of record. Not one of these appointments conflicts with the dates of the five canonical Ripper murders. Either the forger was uncannily lucky or the diary may just have been genuine.

Handwriting experts have declared the writing to be stylistically 'of the period' and the distinctive features to be characteristic of a deranged person. Moreover, these features (such as the crossing of two separated 't's with a single flourish) reappear throughout the diary, which would be difficult for a forger to maintain. On the other hand, the script is wholly unlike that of James Maybrick when compared to his will. Again, advocates of the diary's authenticity have a ready explanation. Maybrick was too ill to write his will and so dictated it to his brother. This scenario is reinforced by the fact that the name of Maybrick's daughter has been misspelled in the will, a mistake a father would never make.

Forensics find the truth

The 'acid test' for any disputed document is, of course, the forensic dating of the paper and ink. In the case of the Ripper diary the British Museum confirmed that the paper did indeed date from the Victorian era (which was never in dispute) and that the fading of the ink was also consistent with its age.

However, powdered Victorian ink can be purchased in many antique stores and, though it may be in a poor state, it can be rendered usable by dilution with water. Ink can also be artificially dated, as the forgers of the Mussolini diaries have shown, by baking it in an oven for 30 minutes.

For many years following the publication of the diary, Ripper scholars were divided between those who accepted its authenticity with reservations and those who dismissed it as a forgery out of hand. It was only when ink samples were subjected to a specific test for the presence of chloroacetamide, a modern preservative, in October 1994 that the truth was finally revealed. The test proved positive. The diary was a fake and Barrett apparently confessed to being its author, though it is possible he only did this to remove the pressure of the publicity to which he was subjected. There are still Ripperologists who contend that the ink test is inconclusive perhaps because, like the general public, they prefer the myth to the facts.

Inside the disturbing mind of Jack the Ripper

It is a disturbing fact that Jack the Ripper was not unique. Two years before the Whitechapel murderer terrorized the East End, the German-born psychoanalyst Richard von Krafft-Ebing published a weighty academic study of sexual perversion detailing many true cases of sadistic sexual murder which bear an uncanny similarity to those perpetrated by the Ripper. Krafft-Ebing's *Psychopathia Sexualis* was intended to prove that there was a scientific basis for all forms of sexual aberration so that the legal and medical authorities could understand the basis of these neuroses and psychoses and learn how to treat those who suffered from them. This influential study was revised and republished many times after its initial publication in 1886, with the Whitechapel case (number 17) added to a later edition. It remains a valued reference work for criminologists and profilers to this day.

'(a) Lust-Murder (Lust Potentiated as Cruelty, Murderous Lust Extending to Anthropophagy).

The most horrible example, and one which most pointedly shows the connection between lust and a desire to kill, is the case of Andreas Bichel, which Feuerbach published in his "Aktenmassige Darstellung merkwurdiger Verbrechen".

He killed and dissected the ravished girls. With reference to one of his victims, at his examination he expressed himself as follows: "I opened her breast and with a knife cut through the fleshy parts of the body. Then I arranged the body as a butcher does beef, and hacked it with an axe into pieces of a size to fit the hole which I had dug up in the mountain

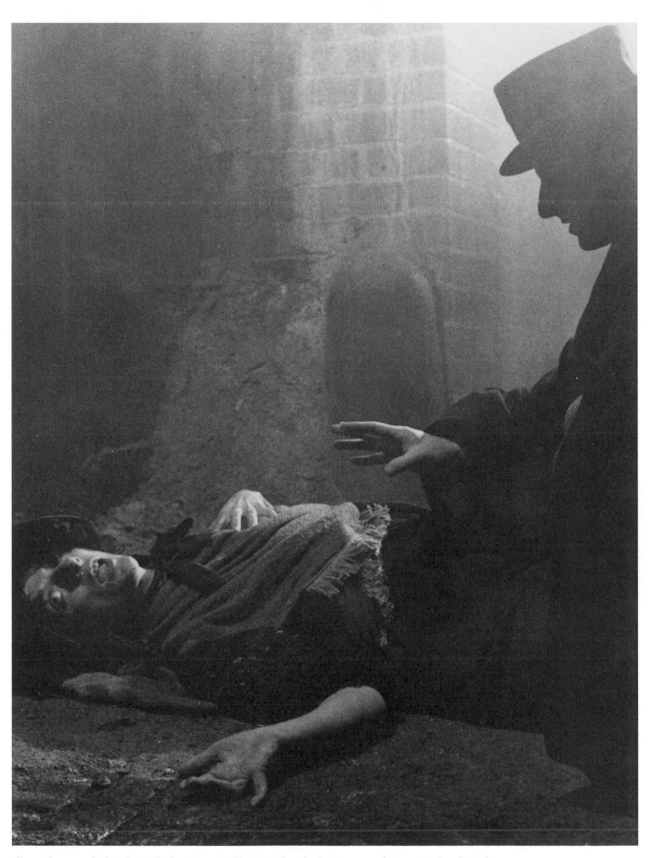

Ill met by moonlight: the Jack the Ripper tableau in the Black Museum of New Scotland Yard

for burying it. I may say that while opening the body I was so greedy that I trembled, and could have cut out a piece and eaten it."

Lombroso, too ("Geschlechtstrieb und Verbrechen in ihren gegenseitigen Beziehungen." Goltdammer's Archiv. Bd. xxx), mentions cases falling in the same category. A certain Philippe indulged in strangling prostitutes, after the sex act, and said: "I am fond of women, but it is sport for me to strangle them after having enjoyed them."

A certain Grassi (Lombroso, op. cit., p. 12) was one night seized with sexual desire for a relative. Irritated by her remonstrance, he stabbed her several times in the abdomen with a knife, and also murdered her father and uncle who attempted to hold him back. Immediately thereafter he hastened to visit a prostitute in order to cool in her embrace his sexual passion. But this was not sufficient, for he then murdered his own father and slaughtered several oxen in the stable.

It cannot be doubted, after the foregoing, that a great number of so-called lust murders depend upon a combination of excessive and perverted desire. As a result of this perverse colouring of the feelings, further acts of bestiality with the corpse may result – e.g., cutting it up and wallowing in the intestines . . .

CASE 17. Jack the Ripper. On December 1, 1887, July 7, August 8, September 30, one day in the month of October and on the 9th of November, *1888; on the Ist of June, the 17th of July and the 10th of September, 1889, the bodies of women were found in various lonely quarters of London ripped open and mutilated in a peculiar fashion. The murderer has never been found. It is probable that he first cut the throats of his victims, then ripped open the abdomen and groped among the intestines. In some instances he cut off the genitals and carried them away; in others he only tore them to pieces and left them behind. He does not seem to have had sexual intercourse with his victims, but very likely the murderous act and subsequent mutilation of the corpse were equivalents for the sexual act.'*

We may think that serial killers are a uniquely modern scourge, but the dozens of similar cases detailed in the *Psychopathia Sexualis* prove that the human capacity for evil has not diminished with our increased understanding of the human mind and ability to treat mental illness.

FBI file: *profiling the Ripper*

In 1988, exactly one hundred years after the Whitechapel murders, two FBI agents drew on their extensive experience of hunting serial killers to compile a psychological profile of Jack the Ripper. Special agents Roy Hazelwood and John Douglas approached the mystery as if it were a modern murder case, stripping away spurious speculation and the confusion created by numerous conspiracy theories to consider the case solely on the facts as recorded in the official police reports.

From the documented evidence, the location of the crime scenes and the nature of the attacks, the agents concluded that Jack was a white male in his mid- to late-twenties and possessed average intelligence. The fact that he went undetected was attributable to luck, not his cunning.

The Ripper was a habitual predatory killer who prowled the streets in anticipation of cornering a likely victim on whom he could indulge his perverted sexual fantasies. There was no pattern to the murders – they were spontaneous, opportunistic slayings. Such killers always stalk the same few streets, like a wild animal which has marked its territory. Had the police known at the time that the killer had a compulsion to repeatedly return to the scene of his crimes they might have been able to catch him in the act.

The Ripper's background

His choice of victim, together with the nature of the mutilations, suggests the Ripper had been raised by a domineering female who is likely to have subjected him to repeated physical and sexual abuse. The effect of this would have been to create a child with

There was no pattern to the murders ... such killers always stalk the same streets, like a wild animal which has marked its territory

sadistic, antisocial impulses, which may have driven him to torture animals and commit arson. Such tendencies would have continued into adult life when the Ripper would have exhibited extreme erratic behaviour, sufficient to provoke his neighbours and arouse the suspicions of the police. Therefore the authorities should have been looking for someone who had previously come to their attention for repeated acts of violence and irrational antisocial behaviour.

The Ripper was evidently single, had probably never married and was unlikely to have any friends. The fact that all the murders took place between midnight and 6am suggests that he was nocturnal by nature, lived alone and had no family responsibilities.

It is a fair assumption that he lived very close to the crime scenes, as predatory killers invariably start by murdering victims close to their homes, and it would appear that he knew the area well enough to carry out his crimes undetected and elude capture after being disturbed.

As for his appearance, he would have had poor personal hygiene and would have looked dishevelled, the very antithesis of the slumming gentleman of leisure cutting through the fog in top hat and cane envisaged in countless

*The women of
the East End
were on the alert*

films and novels. If he was employed it would have been in a menial position and one in which he would have had little or no contact with the public. He was certainly not a professional man and, contrary to popular myth, the mutilations did not demonstrate medical knowledge, or even rudimentary surgical skill.

It is revealing that he subdued and killed his victims quickly as this indicates that the taking of a life was not of primary importance to him. The mutilations are the most significant clue to his state of mind. The murders were clearly sexually motivated and by displacing the victim's sexual organs he was symbolically rendering them sexless and therefore no longer a threat. He clearly hated women and felt intimidated by them.

Using modern profiling techniques, Hazelwood and Douglas eliminated some of the prime suspects, notably Sir William Gull, and point the finger at one specific individual, Kosminski, whom they have confidently identified as Jack the Ripper (see page 114).

CHAPTER 4

THE USUAL SUSPECTS

On the evening of 10 February 1889 a short, neatly dressed man of European appearance walked into a Dundee police station and calmly informed the duty officer that his wife had committed suicide. When the police arrived at his home they found a woman's body with severe injuries to the genitals and bruising around her throat. She had evidently been strangled and mutilated post-mortem. Moreover, the preliminary medical examination revealed that a second set of mutilations had been inflicted some time after the first by a sharp knife. The murderer had clearly returned to inflict more damage to satiate his sadistic appetite.

But that was not all. During their search of the premises the police found two curious messages chalked by a back door. They read 'jack ripper is at the back of this door' and 'jack ripper is in this seller' (sic). Was it possible that the Whitechapel murderer had fled to Scotland for fear that the police were closing in and had his wife been silenced to prevent her revealing that she knew of his crimes?

Further investigation uncovered a trunk containing a belt mottled with old, dried blood and two cheap imitation gold rings of the type that had been torn from Annie Chapman's fingers.

The trial of Jack the Ripper – William Henry Bury (1859–1889)

The name of the man they arrested and charged that night was William Henry Bury. During subsequent questioning detectives teased out more details which convinced them that the man they had in custody was more than just a wife murderer with delusions of notoriety. He matched the description of the Whitechapel murderer given by several key witnesses. A photographic portrait taken in August 1888 shows Bury looking the very image of the man described by PC Smith and witness William Marshall in Berner Street on the day Elizabeth Stride was killed. He also fitted the psychological profile of the Ripper that would be drawn up by FBI profilers a century later.

A psychopathic personality

While still a boy Bury had witnessed his mother hauled off to a lunatic asylum and seen his father torn apart from groin to chin by the wheel of a cart – images which he may have been unconsciously exorcising during the Whitechapel murders. It has been said that Polly Nichols may have been killed simply because she was wearing a jacket with a picture of a man leading a horse, such associations being sufficient to trigger a violent response from a psychopathic personality.

According to contemporary accounts, Bury exhibited all the personality traits that define the psychopathic personality. He was a compulsive liar, a thief and suffered from acute paranoia. He carried knives with him for fear of being attacked and even slept with one under his pillow. He both feared and hated women and is thought to have caught venereal disease, possibly from his wife, Ellen

Elliot, who continued to work as a prostitute despite having inherited £500 which Bury squandered on drink and other vices within a year of their marriage. That same year, 1887, they moved to Bow in London's East End where Bury worked as a horsemeat butcher, a trade in which he could indulge his sadistic fantasies vicariously and perhaps even his need to avenge his father's death, albeit on the carcass of dead animals.

More significantly, inquiries revealed that Bury could not account for his whereabouts on the nights of the East End murders and that he had exhibited signs of extreme agitation, behaving 'like a madman' after returning home on the night Annie Chapman had been killed. Whatever the reason for his unexplained nocturnal walks and bizarre behaviour, it is a fact that he sold his horse and cart in December 1888 shortly after the last Ripper murder and left London with Ellen in January 1889.

Final words

An indication of how seriously the police took the possibility of a 'Ripper' connection can be gleaned from the fact that Scotland Yard sent Inspector Abberline and another detective up to Scotland to assess the evidence and interview Bury in his cell. But Bury refused to confess. Even when the hangman stood before him he remained defiant. 'I suppose you think you are clever to hang me,' snarled Bury with venom. 'But because you are to hang me you are not to get anything out of me.' Evidently he was holding out for a reprieve in exchange for his full confession to the Whitechapel murders.

But was he the Ripper, or was this merely yet another of his warped, self-aggrandising fantasies? Abberline was apparently satisfied and is said to have told the executioner, 'We are quite satisfied that you have hanged Jack the Ripper. There will be no more Whitechapel crimes.' And that, at least, was true.

George Chapman

George Chapman (1865–1903)

Polish-born Severin Antoniovich Klosowski assumed the name of George Chapman in 1895 in a belated attempt to evade the unwanted attentions of the British authorities, who were beginning to suspect him of having murdered several of his former wives. In one of the few surviving photographs, he looks the image of the dapper gent with his long black moustache, but in reality he was a callous, manipulative and violent man with a spiteful streak. But was he Jack the Ripper?

Before emigrating from Poland in the spring of 1887 Klosowski had worked as an assistant to a surgeon in Svolen and so would have possessed the medical skill to have performed the crude operations on each of the Whitechapel victims. However, he must have failed to qualify as a doctor because when he came to England he worked as a lowly barber's assistant. Eventually he owned a barber shop of his own at 126 Cable Street which was within walking distance of all the Whitechapel murder sites.

But by 1890 his business had closed and he was forced to work again as a barber's assistant, this time in a barber shop on the corner of Whitechapel Road and George Yard, only yards from where Martha Tabram had been murdered. In April the following year he and his second wife, Lucy Baderski, emigrated to America, where he continued his philandering ways and when she confronted him with his infidelities he would beat her in a fit of temper. At one point he attacked her with a knife which persuaded Lucy to return to England alone. He followed her and they were temporarily reconciled but eventually separated.

Over the following months he took a series of common-law wives, subjected them to physical abuse and murdered each of them in turn as soon as he had tired of them.

A proven murderer

At his trial in 1903 Chapman was proven to be a serial murderer and clearly capable of sporadic outbursts of violence. However, the main problem with Chapman's candidacy as a Ripper suspect is that he murdered all of his wives by poisoning them and murderers rarely change their *modus operandi*, although it is possible if they believe that they risk capture by continuing their pattern of behaviour. This apparently did not bother Inspector Abberline, who is said to have congratulated his colleague Inspector Godley on Chapman's arrest with the words, 'At last you have captured Jack the Ripper!' Apparently not dissuaded by the fact that Chapman was only 23 years old during the Autumn of Terror, much younger than any of the men that the witnesses had described, Abberline later explained his optimism in an article published in the *Pall Mall Gazette* while Chapman was awaiting execution.

'*I have been so struck with the remarkable coincidences in the two series of murders that I have not been able to think of anything else for several days past – not, in fact, since the Attorney-General made his opening statement at the recent trial, and traced the antecedents of Chapman before he came to this country in 1888. Since then the idea has taken full possession of me, and everything fits in and dovetails so well that I cannot help feeling that this is the man we struggled so hard to capture fifteen years ago . . .*

As I say, there are a score of things which make one believe that Chapman is the man; and you must understand that we have never believed all those stories about Jack the Ripper being dead, or that he was a lunatic, or anything of that kind. For instance, the date of the arrival in England coincides with the beginning of the series of murders in Whitechapel; there is a coincidence also in the fact that the murders ceased in London when Chapman went to America, while similar murders began to be perpetrated in America after he landed there. The fact that he studied medicine and surgery in Russia before he came over here is well established, and it is curious to note that the first series of murders was the work of an expert surgeon, while the recent poisoning cases were proved to be done by a man with more than an elementary knowledge of medicine. The story told by Chapman's wife of the attempt to murder her with a long knife while in America is not to be ignored.

One discrepancy only have I noted, and this is that the people who alleged that they saw Jack the Ripper at one time or another, state that he was a man about thirty-five or forty years of age.

They, however, state that they only saw his back, and it is easy to misjudge age from a back view.

As to the question of the dissimilarity of character in the crimes which one hears so much about, I cannot see why one man should not have done both, provided he had the professional knowledge, and this is admitted in Chapman's case. A man who could watch his wives being slowly tortured to death by poison, as he did, was capable of anything; and the fact that he should have attempted, in such a cold-blooded manner, to murder his first wife with a knife in New Jersey, makes one more inclined to believe in the theory that he was mixed up in the two series of crimes . . . Indeed, if the theory be accepted that a man who takes life on a wholesale scale never ceases his accursed habit until he is either arrested or dies, there is much to be said for Chapman's consistency. You see, [the] incentive changes; but the fiendishness is not eradicated. The victims too, you will notice, continue to be women; but they are of different classes, and obviously call for different methods of despatch.'

Chapman was hanged on 7 April 1903. Other factors in favour of him being the Ripper are that the murders began shortly after he arrived in England and stopped when he left; he had a regular job and was only free at the weekends when the murders took place; and he was known to have been walking the streets of the East End until the early hours. His insatiable sexual drive has been highlighted as a possible motive, but it could prove the opposite as the victims were not sexually assaulted. In fact, their mutilations indicate someone who was sexually inhibited and who could only exorcise his frustration through violence. Witnesses have described seeing a 'foreigner' in the company of some of the victims and this would match Chapman, but others claim to have overheard the supposed killer talking in English, which Chapman couldn't have done at that time as his grasp of English was rudimentary to say the least.

Given all the facts, the case against Chapman is circumstantial at best and it is difficult to see why Abberline was so insistent that the yard had finally got their man.

The doctor and the Devil

Doctor Roslyn D'Onston (real name Robert Donston Stephenson) was what criminologists would today call 'a police buff' – someone who gets a thrill by deliberately bringing themselves to the attention of the investigators, teasing them with misinformation and

> **His insatiable sex drive has been highlighted as a possible motive, but ... the victims were not sexually assaulted**

The only known photograph of Roslyn D'Onston, a self-confessed Satanist who boasted of inside knowledge of the murders

tantalizing clues. For such people the police are a tenacious but unimaginative adversary against whom they believe they can pit their superior intellect. But there was a more sinister side to Dr D'Onston, one which may explain his bravado as an unconscious desire to be caught and thus saved from fulfilling his pact with the Devil.

D'Onston was a self-confessed Satanist who practised black magic and boasted of his inside knowledge of the murders (see page 148). He got a vicarious thrill from the thought that his mistress and close friends believed he was Jack the Ripper. He was also an alcoholic and a drug addict who revelled in the nickname 'Sudden Death', a morbid appellation which persuaded some investigators to consider him a strong suspect in the Whitechapel murders. And he had the opportunity to stalk and kill the victims, as he lived within walking distance of the murder scenes. But what motive might he have had to murder and mutilate five women?

Was it gross arrogance and perverted pride or idle speculation that led him to write an article for the *Pall Mall Gazette* three weeks after the final murder in which he offered a motive for the Ripper killings? By suggesting that the killer had butchered the victims to obtain a heart and body fat for use in black magic rituals was he hoping to divert attention away from his own diabolical practices, or was he unconsciously confessing to the crimes and taunting the police to make the connection? In the article D'Onston described the mutilations in graphic detail and with obvious relish, which suggests that he might have written the piece to satisfy his compulsion to confess and also to boast of what he had got away with. But later he accused a colleague whom the police were able to rule out of their inquiries.

A prime suspect?

It has been suggested that D'Onston may have accused another doctor knowing that he would be proven innocent so that the police would consider D'Onston a harmless eccentric with wild, unsubstantiated theories if his name came up as a suspect in subsequent enquiries, but those who knew Dr D. were not so easily fooled. His mistress, Mabel Collins, later claimed that D'Onston boasted of being Jack the Ripper and allegedly showed her physical evidence of his crimes. Collins subsequently confided her fears in a fellow Theosophist, Vittoria Cremers, who shared an apartment with D'Onston, after which Cremers made a thorough search of his rooms.

What she found there makes a convincing case for his claim to be the Whitechapel murderer: a small metal box containing several neckties encrusted with what appeared to be dried blood. These might have served as macabre tokens of his kills with which he could relive the thrill of the murder, or they may even have played a part in his satanic ceremonies.

D'Onston's value as a prime suspect is strengthened by the fact that the notorious magician Aleister Crowley later took possession of the black box and claimed that it had belonged to Jack the Ripper (see page 153).

As a bizarre postscript to this infernal affair, D'Onston recanted on his pact with the Devil shortly after the final murder and became a devout Christian, devoting the remainder of his days to writing a treatise on the Gospels.

Montague John Druitt (1857–88)

Sir Melville Macnaghten has a lot to answer for. Had he not named Druitt,

Kosminski and Ostrog (see pages 164–70) in his infamous memorandum of 1891, they would never have been considered suspects in the Whitechapel murders. There is no hard evidence for assuming that any of them could have been responsible for the Ripper killings. Druitt was named because his death by drowning in the first week of December 1888 coincided with the end of the series of slayings and because his family suspected him of being the Ripper. It is true that his age at the time of the murders and his respectable appearance matched the descriptions given by several key witnesses, but he was a slight, slender man, not at all like the sturdy, broad-shouldered figure the witnesses described. There is also the matter of location. Druitt lived in Blackheath, not the East End, and it seems unlikely he could have slipped away from the murder scenes bespattered with blood and made his way back to Blackheath by public transport unobserved. Alternatively, he could have stayed overnight in a local lodging house, but his affluent appearance would have aroused suspicion.

Macnaghten, who did not join the Yard until June 1889, betrays his ignorance of the suspects by referring to Druitt as a doctor when in fact he was a barrister and schoolteacher. One can only assume that Macnaghten mistook the initials MD on Druitt's belongings for a medical qualification or perhaps he assumed he had been a doctor as he came from a respected medical family. Either that or he was misled by errors in an earlier report. Whatever the reason, it is a careless mistake which is compounded by other errors – Druitt's age, address and date of death – and assumptions, rendering the memorandum an item of historical interest but of little value to the investigation.

An unlikely candidate

So tenuous is the link between Druitt and the Whitechapel murders that one is tempted to consider the possibility that the real purpose of Macnaghten's report was to submit a short list of candidates on whom the authorities could lay the blame should they be pressured to explain why they had failed to catch the killer.

Macnaghten's suspicions are particularly unjustified in the case of Druitt, who was the son of a doctor, a graduate of Winchester College and an accomplished cricketer. In fact, he played in an important match in Dorset on 1 September, the day after the murder of Polly Nichols, and on 8 September he played at Blackheath only hours after the Annie Chapman murder – something perhaps only a real Dr Jekyll might have been able to pull off convincingly.

There are no reasonable grounds for Macnaghten's assertion that Druitt was 'sexually insane'. His abrupt dismissal from his teaching post at the Blackheath Boarding School for boys just a few weeks before his death may have been due to sexual

Montague Druitt whose own family suspected him of being the Whitechapel murderer

misconduct or his increasingly erratic behaviour which Druitt feared might prove to be the first symptoms of insanity, a condition he was terrified he might have inherited from a member of his family. Druitt's suicide note read: 'Since Friday I felt I was going to be like mother, and the best thing for me was to die.'

There is no hint of dementia in the suicide note, only resignation and despair – not what one would expect from a tormented soul with the blood of five or more women on his hands. Moreover, the typical serial killer is driven by the need to prove his superiority over both his victims and the police. Few are known to have committed suicide, which would be seen as an admission of defeat.

Unfortunately Macnaghten's musings were leaked to influential columnists such as George Robert Sims, who assumed it to be the Yard's official line and so published speculation as fact, thereby adding to the many myths and misconceptions which have obscured the truth more effectively than the proverbial pea-souper London fog. In January 1889 Sims opined:

'I have no doubt a great many lunatics have said they were Jack the Ripper on their death beds. It is a good exit . . . I don't want to interfere . . . but I don't quite see how the real Jack could have confessed seeing that he committed suicide after the horrible mutilation of the woman in the house in Dorset Street,

Spitalfields. The full details of that crime have never been published – they never could be. Jack, when he committed that crime, was in the last stage of the peculiar mania from which he suffered. He had become grotesque in his ideas as well as bloodthirsty. Almost immediately after this murder he drowned himself in the Thames. His name is perfectly well known to the police. If he hadn't committed suicide he would have been arrested.'

Secret misinformation

However, Macnaghten may not have been the only police official to have had suspicions regarding Druitt. In March 1889, Albert Backert, a founder of the Whitechapel Vigilance Committee, demanded to know why the police had recently reduced their presence in the East End and was informed that he would be told the truth if he promised to take an oath of secrecy. He later wrote:

'Foolishly, I agreed. It was then suggested to me that the Vigilance Committee and its patrols might be disbanded as the police were quite certain that the Ripper was dead. I protested that, as I had been sworn to secrecy, I really ought to be given more information than this. "It isn't necessary for you to know any more," I was told. "The man in question is dead. He was fished out of the Thames two months ago and it would only cause pain to relatives if we said any more than that."'

It is not known to whom Backert (an unreliable source) had spoken, but it was certainly not Inspector Abberline, who poured scorn on the whole idea of Druitt having been a serious suspect. In 1903 he told a reporter, 'I know all about that story. But what does it amount to? Simply this. Soon after the last murder in Whitechapel the body of a young doctor was found in the Thames, but there is absolutely nothing beyond the fact that he was found at that time to incriminate him.'

Jill the Ripper

Hammer horror fans may be familiar with *Dr Jekyll And Sister Hyde*, the studio's cheeky re-imagining of R.L. Stevenson's morality tale in which the good doctor's feminine side takes the upper hand and slaughters young Whitechapel women to obtain the hormones needed for her experiments. Implausible though it might sound, Inspector Abberline seriously considered a similar, if less fanciful, line of inquiry at the time of the Ripper murders.

Partly out of sheer frustration but also no doubt driven by the desire to pursue all avenues, no matter how unlikely, Abberline discussed the idea that Jack might be a Jill with colleague Dr Thomas Dutton. Dutton agreed that it was conceivable that a midwife could have possessed sufficient surgical skill to have removed the reproductive organs, but he thought it more likely that a man might have dressed in

Hammer horror: Dr Jekyll and Sister Hyde

women's clothes in order to pass through the streets at night without attracting suspicion – which, incidentally, was a theory favoured by Sir Arthur Conan Doyle. Had Conan Doyle pitched his fictional detective against the Ripper we can assume this is the solution he would have chosen.

A murderous midwife?

Either scenario might explain the discrepancies in the witness statements in the case of the Mary Kelly murder. The police surgeons estimated her time of death as around 4am, but local resident Mrs Caroline Maxwell was adamant that she had seen Kelly between 8 and 8.30 that morning and again an hour later, having recognized her by her clothes, specifically a maroon-coloured shawl that she had seen Kelly wearing on a previous occasion. If Mrs Maxwell had not mistaken the sighting for the day before, and assuming that the police surgeons were correct in estimating time of death, the only other explanation is that the murderer was wearing her clothes. If it was a man he would not have fooled the stranger Mrs Maxwell saw Kelly talking to outside the Prince Albert public house on the second occasion, but another woman in Kelly's clothes might have engaged in conversation to avoid arousing suspicion. That said, it seems more likely that Mrs Maxwell was simply mistaken as to the day, though when Abberline questioned her again she stuck to her story.

A psychopathic midwife might sound absurd, but female serial killers are not unknown and in the East End of the 1880s a female Ripper would have enjoyed certain obvious advantages. She would have been able to move freely through the streets and, if questioned, would be able to explain her presence in the neighbourhood in the early hours of the morning. If she was unfortunate enough to get bloodstains on her clothing that too could be explained away.

Method and motive

In 1939 William Stewart was the first to speculate that the killer might be a woman in his book *Jack the Ripper: A New Theory*. His theory hinged on the answer to four crucial questions:

1. Who could walk the street at night without arousing suspicion or having to explain their movements to friends or family?
2. Who would have a viable reason for wearing bloodstained clothing?
3. Who would have had the skill to perform the crude operations in near darkness at speed and under stress?
4. Who might have been able to extricate themselves from suspicion if discovered leaning over the body?

But if it was a woman, what motive could she have had?

Stewart considered the possibility that she might have been an abortionist and if so, she may have been betrayed by a married woman whom she had tried to help which would have meant a prison sentence. The Whitechapel murders might therefore have been her revenge. In support of this theory it should be reiterated that no one heard the victims cry out, which could be explained by the fact that midwives who worked among the poor were apparently trained to induce unconsciousness in intoxicated or violent patients by exerting pressure on the nerve centres around the collar bone.

The main problem with the mad midwife scenario, however, is that there is no obvious connection between the victims and their murderer. Mary Kelly was the only victim who was pregnant at the time of her death. Stewart also ignores the testimony of Albert Cadosch, who claimed to have heard a man and woman conversing on the other side of the fence in the backyard of 29 Hanbury Street three minutes before something fell against the fence where the body of Annie Chapman was later found.

In support of his scenario Stewart raises the spectre of Mary Pearcey, who in October 1890 murdered her lover's wife and child by cutting their throats and then wheeling their bodies in a barrow to a deserted street, where she dumped them. For those who doubt that a woman would have the strength to sever a throat with the force with which the Ripper despatched his victims Sir Melville Macnaghten said of Pearcey, 'I have never seen a woman of stronger physique . . . her nerves were as iron cast as her body.' A curious footnote to the case can be found in the fact that shortly before her execution Pearcey asked for a notice to be placed in a Spanish newspaper which read, 'M.E.C.P. last wish of M.E.W. Have not betrayed.' No doubt the conspiracy theorists will have much pleasure in speculating to whom those initials refer.

He was dirty and dishevelled ... He cut a pathetic figure. No prostitute would have touched him ...

The lunatic fringe – Aaron Kosminski (1865–1919) and Michael Ostrog (1833–?)

Kosminski, by all accounts, was an even less likely suspect than Druitt. Macnaghten only named him because he was Swanson and Anderson's chief suspect although there is no hard evidence to connect him. Again, Macnaghten passes judgment based on crucial errors and assumptions. Kosminski was indeed incarcerated in Colney Hatch asylum shortly after the cessation of the murders in 1891. However, he did not die soon afterwards as Macnaghten states – he was committed in 1894 – but 28 years later, during which time he did not commit any crimes or exhibit any signs of serious violence. In fact, he was a docile imbecile for most of his life and could not have been responsible for the brutal attacks which Macnaghten suspected him of. He had been a familiar figure in the East End, where he scavenged for scraps of food in the gutter and complained of hearing voices in his head. He was dirty and dishevelled, not the man of 'shabby genteel' appearance the witnesses had described. He cut a pathetic figure. No prostitute would have touched him and he would have been unaware of their presence.

The official file at Colney Hatch describes Kosminski as being 'apathetic as a rule' and 'incoherent'. On only one occasion was he recorded as having threatened a member of staff with violence. If one thing can be stated with certainty, it is that Kosminski would not have been found guilty if he was on trial today.

A *habitual offender*

The third suspect named by Macnaghten was a habitual thief and a compulsive liar, but there is no evidence to suggest that he ever killed anyone. Again, there is a nagging

Michael Ostrog

suspicion that he appears in the memorandum merely to give the impression that the police had their eye on a number of men whom they could have called in for questioning at any time, when in fact they had no definite leads at all.

Michael Ostrog, a Russian immigrant, had a police record stretching back to 1863, when he was arrested in Oxford for burglary under the alias Max Gosslar and sentenced to ten months' hard labour. On his release, he travelled to Bishop's Stortford, where he conned money from several of the more trusting inhabitants while posing as a Polish aristocrat until he was unmasked as a fraud and sentenced to a further three months' imprisonment.

The next entry in his police file is dated July 1866, when he was sentenced to seven years' penal servitude for theft. He was released in May 1873, only to reoffend six months later when he received a ten-year sentence. In September 1887 he was certified insane, following an incident in which he had tried to commit suicide by jumping in front of a train while handcuffed to a police escort.

A *suspect vanishes*

Less than six months later Ostrog was discharged and roaming the streets of Whitechapel during the 'Autumn of Terror', presumably no saner than he had been before his confinement in the asylum. On 26 October he was listed as being at large for failing to report at a police station as a condition of his release and was listed as 'dangerous'. Yet he had exhibited no signs of violence other than the desire to die under the wheels of a train in the company of a gaoler.

It can only be assumed that he fitted the profile of the Ripper – a mentally unstable individual who had boasted of having rudimentary medical training. But his subsequent behaviour contradicts Macnaghten's assessment that he was a 'homicidal maniac'. He was arrested in 1891 and again in 1894 for petty theft, but on neither occasion did the police take the opportunity to charge him with the Whitechapel murders. On his release from prison in 1904 he vanished and was never heard of again.

Two strong candidates: James Kelly (1860–1929) and 'GWB'

There is no evidence to connect wife-murderer James Kelly with Ripper victim Mary Kelly, but on the morning after Mary's murder the police raided James Kelly's lodgings only to discover that he had fled to Dieppe. Two days later, on 12 November, a police official whose initials were CET added a note to James Kelly's file querying what steps had been taken to arrest him, although it is not clear whether this was in reference to his wife's murder or the Whitechapel murders in general. The timing may have been purely coincidental. However, it is known that Inspector Monro took a keen interest in the whereabouts of James Kelly, who

had been diagnosed a paranoid schizophrenic in Broadmoor Lunatic Asylum from which he had escaped in January 1888. Kelly had murdered his wife because he believed she had infected him with venereal disease, but during his stay in Broadmoor he became convinced that he had caught it from the whores of Whitechapel. Unfortunately, after his escape from the asylum his movements are unknown. He may have been lodging in Whitechapel and exercising revenge on the prostitutes who he blamed for infecting him, or he may have gone to ground elsewhere in an effort to evade the police who had a warrant for his arrest. There is no way of knowing for certain, but he remains a strong candidate.

'GWB' – an old man's confession

The late Daniel Farson was one of the most respected Ripper scholars, whose most celebrated coup was the rediscovery of the Macnaghten Memoranda. His reputation made him an obvious clearing house for every crackpot theory regarding the Ripper, but one item of correspondence that he received in 1959 had an air of authenticity which he found difficult to dismiss.

The letter was sent from Australia by a man who signed himself 'GWB'. In it, he told of his childhood in London's East End during the late-1880s when his mother would chide him to come inside by calling, 'Come in, Georgie, or Jack the Ripper will get you.' On one occasion his father, a drunken brute, patted his son on the head and assured the boy that he would be the last person the Ripper would touch.

His father grew increasingly violent, beating Georgie's mother so frequently that father and son stopped speaking to each other for many years. One evening in 1902, Georgie attempted a reconciliation with his father before sailing for Australia. It was then that the old man admitted that he had taken to drink in despair after having fathered a mentally retarded daughter, Georgie's only sister. Having got that off his chest, the old man evidently felt that the moment was right to unburden himself of another secret and confessed to his son that he was guilty of the Whitechapel murders.

He explained that whenever he was violently drunk and the mood would take him he would seek out prostitutes and gut them with a sharp knife, avoiding the risk of getting blood on his clothes by wearing a second pair of trousers over his regular clothes which he would dispose of in the manure he was paid to deliver during the day.

A confession withheld

The old man urged Georgie to change his name when he reached Australia as he had made up his mind to go to the police and make a full statement before his death, but although the boy did as his father told him to the old man appears not to have been able to summon up the courage to confess.

Farson was of the opinion that the story was so simple and credible that it may just have been true. The father appeared to fit the description submitted by Lawende, who saw the murderer at Mitre Square, when the father would have been 38. But how seriously can one take the confession of a drunkard who had failed to make anything of himself and might have been merely bragging to impress his son, or perhaps to spite him by leaving the boy with the belief that he wouldn't amount to anything as he had come from tainted stock?

Portrait of a killer – Walter Sickert (1860–1942)

Interest in the Whitechapel murders has recently been rekindled as a result of the publicity surrounding crime novelist Patricia Cornwell's personally financed investigation into the killings for her book *Portrait Of A Killer*. Cornwell is said to have spent $4 million of her own money to obtain original historical documents and to fund private scientific analysis of DNA specimens which she claims prove that the Victorian painter Walter Sickert was the Ripper. Ripperologists contend that her theory is fanciful in the extreme, that the science is inconclusive and that her deductions are fundamentally flawed.

The idea that Sickert might have

An unhealthy obsession with the seamier side of London life: artist Walter Sickert often used prostitutes as models

been the Ripper was first advanced by author Donald McCormick in his study *The Identity of Jack the Ripper* (1959), expanded upon by Stephen Knight in *Jack the Ripper: The Final Solution* (1976) and made the subject of Jean Overton Fuller's *Sickert and the Ripper Crimes* (1990) as well as Melvyn Fairclough's *Ripper and the Royals* (2002). All five authors based their argument on the belief that Sickert had an unhealthy obsession with the seamier aspect of London life and the Whitechapel murders in particular and also that he used prostitutes as models. But the fact of the matter is that nearly all artists of the period paid prostitutes to model for them as they had no reservations about removing their clothes and they were readily available in the bohemian areas where the artists had their studios.

Sickert found inspiration in the bustle of the music halls and cafés, as had his French Impressionist friends whose style he had adopted. A basic knowledge of Sickert's technique reveals that what might appear to be mutilations in the faces of his figures are simply the result of his spontaneous Impressionistic stylings and have no sinister meaning.

The inspiration for the series of morbid 'Camden Town' paintings was not the Whitechapel murders, but the murder of Emily Dimmock in 1907 which Sickert was familiar with, being a resident of the area at the time. The claim that Mary Kelly, the Ripper's last victim, was the subject for this series of morbid paintings appears to have been yet another after-dinner yarn spun by Joseph Gorman Sickert, the creator of the equally fanciful royal conspiracy tale (see page 142). Gorman claims to be Walter's illegitimate son, but has offered no conclusive proof of his parentage.

Scenes of crime?

Walter Sickert's obsession with the Ripper appears to have originated around the same time as his landlady had shared her suspicions regarding a medical student who had been her lodger at the time of the Whitechapel murders. Much has been made of the fact that Sickert was in the habit of dressing as the Ripper, but he was also known to dress up as other historical and fictional characters. It was an expression of his eccentricity and perhaps a habit left over from his earlier life as an actor.

A more serious accusation is that Sickert included details in his paintings which only the murderer would have known. Here we venture into the murky world of the conspiracy theorist who sees hidden meanings where none were intended, but there is nothing in Sickert's paintings which has any direct bearing on the Ripper murders. Cornwell calls attention to the similarity between the positioning of the models in Sickert's paintings and the position of the bodies at the crime scenes, but Mary Kelly was the only victim photographed at the crime scene. The other women were photographed at the mortuary. As for Cornwell's assertion that a pearl necklace worn by one of Sickert's models was symbolic of blood droplets, the less said the better.

As for a motive, Cornwell claims Sickert was rendered sterile by the appearance of a fistula on his penis and so took his frustration out on prostitutes. But Sickert was a notorious 'immoralist . . . with a swarm of children of provenances which are not possible to count', commented his friend Jacques-Emile Blanche. And the fistula was mere family hearsay, according to his nephew John Lessore.

Sickert may have been an eccentric and later suffered depression but he was not a psychopath. As a letter to Jacques-Emile Blanche reveals, he did not have

Certain Ripperologists 'read' Sickert's paintings for clues to his past. This one, from 1932, is called 'Woman's Sphere'.

an all-consuming hatred of prostitutes. Quite the contrary. 'From 9 to 4, it is an uninterrupted joy, caused by these pretty, little, obliging models who laugh and unembarrassingly be themselves while posing like angels. They are glad to be there, and are not in a hurry.'

Suspect science

The cornerstone of Cornwell's case is that her team of forensic scientists discovered a sequence of mitochondrial DNA (mtDNA) on several 'Ripper letters' which matched DNA recovered from letters written by Sickert. The first problem with this assertion is that there is no proof that the letters received by Scotland Yard in 1888 were written by the Ripper. Quite the contrary. Various high-ranking police officials have stated that they believe the two most infamous letters, the 'Dear Boss' letter and the 'Saucy Jack' postcard, to be a hoax perpetrated by a journalist who had abused his access to inside information and was known to them by name.

The second problem with this particular line of inquiry is that many people have handled both the 'Ripper' and Sickert letters over the course of the past 125 years which, as any forensic expert knows, could have seriously compromised the evidence, rendering them practically useless for proving anything. In fact, the original nuclear DNA tests came back negative and Cornwell's team were forced to rely on mtDNA testing which only

suggested a possible link. However, mtDNA is a less rigorous test and many individuals can share a similar molecular sequence. These sequences are not unique. On Cornwell's own admission, as many as 400,000 people might have shared that particular molecular pattern in Victorian England. Without a sample of DNA taken from Sickert himself or one of his direct descendants no conclusive link can be established and nothing can be stated for certain. For all we know Sickert might have used a sponge to moisten the stamps and seal the envelopes as was a common practice at the time or, as is suspected, a servant might have posted his letters.

In total, 600 letters purporting to be from the killer remain in the police archives (many hundreds more were destroyed). So it is quite likely that with such a large sampling to choose from there is a good chance that one or two letters might have residual DNA that would be a reasonably close match to a specific suspect. But to identify and convict an individual, forensic science demands a positive match – a reasonable proportion of similar characteristics is not sufficient proof. Furthermore, the 'Ripper letter' which Patricia Cornwell claims contains both Sickert's DNA and a watermark found in his own writing paper was never considered a genuine letter by students of the case. So the worst that could be said of Sickert is that he may have been guilty of writing hoax Ripper letters to the police, which does not make him the killer.

An artist abroad

But the most damning evidence against Cornwell's imaginative theory is the fact that Sickert, it appears, was not in London during the time of the murders, but in France. On 6 September 1888, Sickert's mother wrote describing how much Walter and his brother Bernhard were enjoying their holiday in St Valery-en-Caux, and on 16 September Jacques-Emile Blanche wrote to his father describing a congenial visit he had made to Walter there. On 21 September Walter's wife Ellen wrote to her brother-in-law stating that her husband had been holidaying in France for several weeks.

Even allowing for the fact that Walter Sickert was wealthy enough to travel to and from England on the ferry as Cornwell suggests, it seems ludicrous even to consider the possibility that he absented himself from a holiday in France to return to Whitechapel to murder prostitutes whose company he evidently enjoyed and then add obscure clues in his paintings as a boast or confession. What it does prove is that Jack the Ripper continues to intrigue us and will no doubt do so for many more years to come.

A prime suspect – Francis Tumblety (1833–1903)

In 1993, while making a final inventory of his stock, retiring Surrey bookshop owner Eric Barton came across a bundle of letters relating to the Whitechapel murders. His initial feeling was that they were mere curiosities of the period and of as little value as the hundreds of hoax letters received by Scotland Yard during the autumn of 1888. He considered tossing them into the dustbin, but fortunately thought better of it and instead offered them to Suffolk police constable Stewart Evans, who had been a keen collector of Ripper memorabilia since his teens. Evans immediately saw the significance of one particular piece of correspondence written 25 years after the murders by Detective John George Littlechild to journalist George Sims, in

Francis Tumblety

which Littlechild named a prime suspect whom Evans had never heard of before, one whose activities and profile appeared to fit the Ripper profile perfectly – Dr Francis Tumblety. The Littlechild letter has been verified as genuine by forensic experts and no one is disputing its authenticity.

'Knowing the great interest you take in all matters criminal, and abnormal, I am just going to inflict one more letter on you on the "Ripper" subject. Letters as a rule are only a nuisance when they call for a reply but this does not need one. I will try and be brief.

I never heard of a Dr D. in connection with the Whitechapel murders but amongst the suspects, and to my mind a very likely one, was a Dr. T. (which sounds much like D.) He was an American quack named Tumblety and was at one time a frequent visitor to London and on these occasions constantly brought under the notice of police, there being a large dossier concerning him at Scotland Yard. Although a "Sycopathia Sexualis" subject he was not known as a "Sadist" (which the murderer unquestionably was) but his feelings toward women were remarkable and bitter in the extreme, a fact on record. Tumblety was arrested at the time of the murders in connection with unnatural offences and charged at Marlborough Street, remanded on bail, jumped his bail, and got away to Boulogne. He shortly left Boulogne and was never heard of afterwards. It was

believed he committed suicide but certain it is that from this time the "Ripper" murders came to an end.'

It was only by a quirk of fate that Tumblety, an Irish-American, had come to the attention of Inspector Littlechild, who was then investigating Irish Nationalist terror activities on the British mainland. Tumblety had no interest in politics. The only interest he served was his own. A rabid egomaniac and shameless self-publicist, he was wanted in the USA and Canada for posing as a doctor and peddling patent medicines of dubious merit, some of them allegedly lethal. The only known photograph shows him sporting a military-style uniform to which he was certainly not entitled.

Morbid interests

The finger of suspicion begins to point towards Tumblety when one recalls that the assistant curator of a London pathological museum claimed that he had been approached by an American doctor who had expressed interest in purchasing women's sexual organs and was prepared to pay £20 for each specimen. As Littlechild noted in his letter to Sims, the police considered Tumblety a 'psychopathia sexualis' rather than a sadist. He may have simply had a morbid interest in collecting such objects, but his unhealthy obsession nevertheless makes him a more likely suspect than the suicidal Druitt, the harmless

Chief Inspector Littlechild

Elizabeth Stride's body was found and is just ten minutes' walk from the other murder sites, less than five if one is running. At the height of the panic there were rumours that a bloodstained shirt had been discovered in a Whitechapel boarding house and that it belonged to a lodger who had been seen by his landlady returning late at night bespattered with gore.

Although the incident had been widely reported in the national and provincial press at the time, modern researchers have either overlooked it or chosen to dismiss it out of hand as yet another lurid story whipped up by Victorian reporters eager to keep the story spinning – but it has since been confirmed that the house at 22 Batty Street was under surveillance. It is thought that the suspect may have realized that he was being watched and taken up residence elsewhere – namely the Charing Cross Hotel, where a suspicious black bag was later abandoned by a guest who fled the country just after the Ripper murder spree had come to an abrupt end.

After the bag had been advertised in the lost property columns to no avail, the hotel handed it to the police who made an inventory of its contents. Inside they found clothes, cheque books and pornographic prints. The cheque books led the police to cable the American authorities requesting samples of Tumblety's handwriting, suggesting that Tumblety may have been both the owner of the black bag

imbecile Kosminski or the semi-invalid Sir William Gull (see page 147).

Further clues push Tumblety's name to the very top of the list of prime suspects in the Ripper killings. Littlechild's correspondent, the journalist George Sims, had been in Whitechapel at the time of the murders and some years later was approached by a woman who suspected that her lodger may have been the 'Whitechapel fiend'. She had never learnt his name, only that he claimed to be an American doctor. The lodging house in question was at 22 Batty Street, which runs parallel to Berner Street where

and possibly even the mysterious Batty Street lodger. But just as the case appeared to be drawing to a conclusion the British press fell suspiciously silent and the police were equally unforthcoming. Had the press been pressured to drop the story to save Scotland Yard further embarrassment after having let their prime suspect slip through their fingers?

Chase across the Atlantic

The *New York World* revealed that Tumblety had actually been arrested by the London police on 7 November, two days before the last Ripper murder, and charged with gross indecency. But they couldn't hold him for what was legally no more than a misdemeanour. As soon as he was released on bail Tumblety fled first to France then returned to the USA.

Scotland Yard must have realized the enormity of their error, for they rapidly despatched a senior detective and two colleagues across the Atlantic in hot pursuit.

They must have taken the possibility of Tumblety being the Ripper seriously, otherwise they would not have wasted such a valuable resource to recapture someone accused of a simple misdemeanour.

When Tumblety arrived in New York on 4 December 1888 looking 'pale and excited' according to contemporary accounts, he was met by two American detectives and surrounded by noisy newspapermen who wanted to know if he would confess to being Jack the Ripper. They had already questioned his family and acquaintances, most of whom unhesitatingly agreed that the man they knew could be capable of murder. But Tumblety evidently had no intention of being brought to account and fled his lodgings just two days after arriving in New York. Cheated of a good scoop, the most tenacious reporters left for Tumblety's hometown of Rochester in upstate New York, where they tracked down his former neighbours. One remembered the young son of Irish immigrants selling pornography to the men working on the nearby canal. Another revealed that Tumblety used to work as a porter at the local hospital where, it is assumed, he picked up a grasp of medical knowledge which had given him a veneer of credibility.

Gruesome trophies

But Tumblety's medical practice was not confined to peddling patent medicines. He is known to have attempted at least one crude abortion on a gullible prostitute and to have had a bizarre compulsion for collecting medical specimens. A gentleman acquaintance related a disturbing incident to an American reporter which may provide a motive for the hideous crimes Tumblety is accused of having committed in Whitechapel.

'Someone asked why he hadn't invited any women to his dinner. His face

instantly became as black as a thundercloud . . . He said, "I don't know any such cattle. But if I did I would, as your friend, sooner give you a dose of quick poison than to take you into such danger." He then broke into a homily on the sin and folly of dissipation, fiercely denounced all women, especially fallen women. He then invited us into his office to illustrate his lecture, so to speak.'

The guests found themselves in a room brimming with a multitude of anatomical specimens preserved in glass jars including the wombs of 'every class of women'. Could these have been trophies of his victims? And if so, what might have driven him to murder?

A focus for anger

Tumblety is thought to have been bisexual. It was only when he discovered that his wife had been a prostitute and that she continued to ply her trade during their marriage that he turned against all women and indulged in 'unnatural vices'.

One would not expect a man with homosexual leanings to vent his anger on women, but rather on men, whom he might see as having 'corrupted' him. However, it is not inconceivable that Tumblety might have focused his anger on women in the belief that his wife's rejection had forced him to seek the company of men.

And it is surely no coincidence that he committed his first indecency offence on the day of the first Whitechapel murder and that his subsequent offences coincided with the other killings. If he had been filled with self-loathing he might have attempted to exorcise his anger on a vulnerable target – the prostitutes who were substitutes for his wife.

He acquired a basic knowledge of abortions at the Rochester Infirmary, which would have enabled him to remove the organs within minutes and he is known to have collected such specimens. It is also possible that he might have used his rudimentary medical knowledge, respectable appearance and powers of persuasion to pass himself off as a doctor or even a back-street abortionist in the East End to obtain his victims' confidence.

Whatever his methods, it is a matter of record that the Whitechapel murders began when he arrived in England and ceased shortly after he left. The accumulation of circumstantial evidence is compelling, but there is one final fact that might seem to seal the case against Francis Tumblety. When he died in St Louis in 1903, an inventory was made of his possessions. It included the expensive accessories one might expect such a flamboyant figure to possess – a gold pocket watch, jewellery and such. But there were two items which puzzled the nuns who had tended him during his final days: two imitation gold rings worth no more than $3 the pair. Could these have been the rings torn from the dead fingers of Annie Chapman?

The royal conspiracy

Investigative journalist Stephen Knight titled his convoluted conspiracy study of the Whitechapel murders *Jack the Ripper: The Final Solution*. Subsequent research has proved that it was nothing of the kind. It was pure fiction, but for various reasons Knight's dark romance captured the public imagination and has stubbornly refused to be displaced by the sordid, unvarnished facts.

The germ of Knight's story took root in 1973 during research for a BBC docudrama which promised to provide a final solution to the mystery and reveal the identity of Jack the Ripper. Researchers initially approached an unnamed source in Scotland Yard who mentioned that there was a new theory going the rounds concerning a secret marriage between Prince Albert Victor, grandson of Queen Victoria, and an impoverished East End girl named Alice Mary Crook. The source suggested that the researchers should contact Joseph Sickert, who claimed to be the illegitimate son of the painter Walter Sickert and to be privy to the true story behind the Whitechapel murders.

According to Joseph Sickert, Prince Albert Victor – HRH the Duke of Clarence, known to his associates as 'Prince Eddy' – was in the habit of slumming in the East End with Sickert senior as his guide. During one particular sojourn among his less privileged subjects, he became infatuated with a lowly shop assistant, a girl by the name of Annie Crook. Annie was not only from a lower class but she was also a Catholic, which would mean that this Cinderella story could never have had a happy ending. But it was doomed the moment the Queen learned that the prince had fathered an illegitimate child and that he had married Annie in a secret ceremony in the hope of making their relationship official.

A dangerous scandal

If news of the relationship reached the newspapers it would cause more than a scandal – it could precipitate a revolution and bring down both the government and the monarchy. Cracks had already been appearing in the Empire's foundations ever since Sir Charles Warren had ordered the merciless suppression of protestors in Trafalgar Square on 'Bloody Sunday', 13 November 1887. The unemployed were dossing down in Hyde Park and a mob had rampaged through the Mall throwing stones through the windows of gentlemen's clubs. The Establishment was clearly a target for the disenfranchised, disenchanted and dispossessed. The Whitechapel Vigilance Committee and the so-called yellow press (popular papers) were demanding social reforms to make the streets safe from criminals in the wake of the Ripper killings. One more

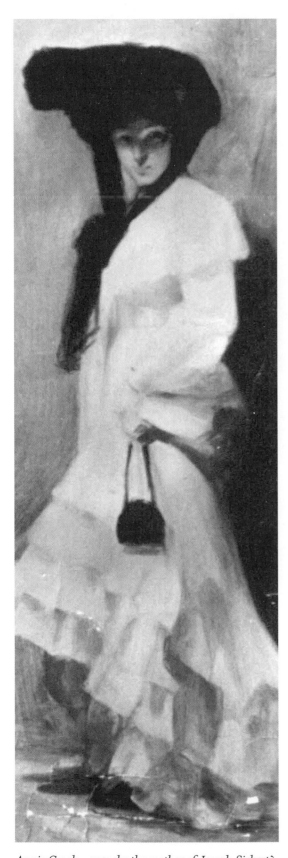

Annie Crook – was she the mother of Joseph Sickert?

provocation and the working class might just take to the streets with clubs, bricks and broken bottles to set the eye of the Empire ablaze.

Something drastic had to be done to smother the story before a journalist caught a sniff. In desperation the Queen entrusted the situation to the Prime Minister, Lord Salisbury. According to Sickert, this loyal servant of the crown sent government agents to abduct the prince and his paramour from their Cleveland Street love nest and confine Annie in an asylum where no one would listen seriously to her tale of a royal plot. However, their plans for the child were thwarted by Annie, who had entrusted the child to the safekeeping of her friend, a prostitute by the name of Mary Kelly. At this point Jack the Ripper makes his entrance upon the stage in opera cloak and black silk top hat like a music-hall villain to despatch Kelly and the small circle of 'working girls' to whom she had entrusted the secret, these being Polly Nichols, Liz Stride and Annie Chapman. Then in the final act he tortures Mary Kelly, who dies refusing to reveal the whereabouts of the child.

Strange theories

A dark fairy tale indeed with obvious elements lifted from Cinderella and Snow White with Queen Victoria cast in the role of the wicked stepmother. But who was the Ripper? Sickert claims it was Sir William Gull, the Queen's personal physician, who enticed the

unfortunate women into his coach with bunches of grapes, disembowelled them in the carriage then dumped the bodies in the streets with the aid of a sycophantic servant, John Netley. As for the mutilations, they were perversions of a fictional Masonic ritual symbolizing the murder of Abrim Abif, the founder of the Freemasons, by three fellow masons, Jubela, Jubelo, and Jubelum – the 'Juwes' named in the Goulston Street graffiti.

The choice of murder sites also had Masonic significance. Mitre Square was reputedly the location of key Masonic lodges and the name itself had Masonic connotations – a mitre and a square being symbols in Masonic ritual. But

this is yet another example of the selective choice of clues. There was also a suspicion that the murderer may have been a Jewish zealot who slaughtered his victims in a ritual sacrifice to his God during the Jewish sabbath. However, the sabbath begins at sunset on a Friday and ends at sunset on Saturday, and since several victims were killed in the early hours of Sunday morning this makes a nonsense of the whole idea.

The story gains currency

Incredibly, the BBC swallowed Sickert's ridiculous story, partly because they could verify a few of the more salient points, such as the fact that a woman named

Princess May and Prince Albert, the Duke of Clarence, each looking the very picture of Victorian respectability

Sir William Gull, physician to Queen Victoria and suspected of the Ripper murders though he was 72 years old at the time

Annie Crook had lived in Cleveland Street at the time and that she had given birth to an illegitimate daughter, but the main reason they endorsed the charade was simply because it made such a rattling good yarn.

And the thing about conspiracies is that the lack of physical evidence is no problem. Quite the opposite, since it can be argued that the conspirators destroyed everything that might implicate them. It is a revisionist historian's dream, but it has no basis in reality.

At this point author Stephen Knight picked up the story. He interviewed Sickert at length and expanded on the 'evidence' unearthed by the BBC, claiming to have obtained access to previously unpublished Scotland Yard files which were not to be open to the public until 1992. According to Knight the masons chose a scapegoat to cover their tracks, a young barrister named Montague Druitt, whom they murdered and offered his body in atonement for the crimes. But just when credulity has been stretched so thin it threatens to snap we are asked to believe that the baby girl survived and grew up to marry none other than Walter Sickert, the man who 20 years earlier had accompanied Prince Albert Victor in his sojourns into Whitechapel!

The real facts

Since the publication of Knight's book researchers have produced documentation which proved that Annie Crook was not confined in an asylum but admitted herself to various workhouses and that during that time she had her baby, Alice Margaret, with her. Furthermore, on her marriage certificate she listed the father of the child as William Crook, who was her grandfather, which suggests her plight originated from incest, not from her involvement with an aristocrat.

As for Sir William Gull being unmasked as the Whitechapel murderer, he suffered a serious stroke in October 1887 which left him partially paralysed. Moreover, he was 72 years old at the time of the Ripper murders which not only doesn't tie in with the witness descriptions, but also makes it unlikely that he would have had the strength to subdue his victims even allowing for the fact that one or two may have been the worse for drink. It also has to be pointed out that none of the residents living at or near the murder sites reported hearing a carriage rattling along the cobblestones in the early hours of the morning which would surely have aroused their suspicion.

And finally there is a further twist to the story that even Stephen Knight could not have come up with: shortly after the publication of *Jack the Ripper: the Final Solution*, Joseph Sickert confessed to the *Sunday Times* that he had fabricated the entire story.

CHAPTER 5 | THE DEVIL MADE HIM DO IT

Of the many hundreds of articles published during the Ripper's reign of terror there were two which bear closer examination, if only because they were penned by the most colourful characters of the age – the notorious occultist Aleister Crowley and the self-confessed Satanist Roslyn D'Onston, who was himself a suspect. The first is by D'Onston, who claims to have identified the murderer's nationality and motive and also speculates that the murder sites may have been chosen in order to form a figure of mystical significance.

The Whitechapel Demon's Nationality: and Why He Committed the Murders

by One Who Thinks He Knows

'It will be remembered that a chalk inscription (which it is not denied was written by the murderer) was found on the wall in Mitre-square, just above the body of the murdered woman. It ran as follows: "The Juwes are the men who will not be blamed for nothing", and was evidently intended to throw suspicion on the Jews. This writing was seen by the police by means of artificial light, and was unfortunately obliterated by them before daylight. Hinc illae lachrymae!! [From hereon they will weep!)

Why did the murderer spell the word Jews "Juwes"? Was it that he was an uneducated Englishman who did not know how to spell the word; was he in reality an ignorant Jew, reckless of consequences and glorying in his deeds; or was he a foreigner, well accustomed to the English language, but who in the tremendous hurry of the moment unconsciously wrote the fatal word in his native tongue?

The answers to these three queries, on

The writing on the wall: the graffiti at Goulston Street really caught hold of the public imagination

which the whole matter rests, are easy. *Juwes* is a much too difficult word for an uneducated man to evolve on the spur of the moment, as any philologist will allow. Any ignorant Jew capable of spelling the rest of the sentence as correctly as he did, would know, certainly, how to spell the name of his own people. Therefore, only the last proposition remains, which we shall now show, in the most conclusive manner, to be the truth.

To critically examine an inscription of this kind, the first thing we naturally do is not to rest satisfied with reading it in print, but to make, as nearly as we can, a facsimile of it in script, thus:-

Juwes

Inspection at once shows us, then, that a dot has been overlooked by the constable who copied it, as might easily occur, especially if it were placed at some distance, after the manner of foreigners.

Juives

Therefore we place a dot above the third upstroke in the word *Juwes*, and we find it to be *Juives*, which is the French word for *Jews* . . . The murderer is, therefore, a Frenchman.

It may here be argued that both Swiss and Belgians make French almost their mother tongue; but Flemish is the natural and usual vehicle for the latter, while the idiosyncrasy of both those nationalities is adverse to this class of crime.

On the contrary, in France, the murdering of prostitutes has long been practised, and has been considered to be almost peculiarly a French crime.

Again, the grammatical construction of the sentence under examination is distinctly French in two points – first, in the double negative contained; and, secondly, in the employment of the definite article before the second noun. An Englishman or an American would have said, "The Jews are men who, &c." But the murderer followed his native idiom "Les Juifs sont des homes" in his thoughts, and when putting it into English rendered des homes "the men".

Again, neither Belgians nor Swiss entertain any animosity to the Jews, whereas the hatred of the French proletarian to them is notorious.

The ground for research being thus cleared and narrowed, the next question is, what is the motive? . . .

Now, in one of the books by the great modern occultist who wrote under the nom de plume of "Eliphaz Levy", "Le Dogme et Rituel de la Haute Magie," we find the most elaborate directions for working magical spells of all kinds. The second volume has a chapter on Necromancy, or black magic, which the author justly denounces as a profanation. Black magic employs the agencies of evil spirits and demons, instead of the beneficent spirits directed by the adepts of la haute magie [High Magic]. At the same time he gives the clearest and fullest details of the necessary steps for evocation by this means, and it is in the list of substances prescribed as absolutely necessary to success that we find the link which joins modern French necromancy with the quest of the East-end murderer. These substances are in themselves horrible, and difficult to procure. They can only be obtained by means of the most appalling crimes, of which murder and mutilation of the dead are the least heinous. Among them are strips of the skin of a suicide, nails from a murderer's gallows, candles made from human fat, the head of a black cat which has been fed forty days on human flesh, the horns of a goat which has been made the instrument of an infamous capital crime, and a preparation made from a certain portion of the body of a harlot. This last point is insisted upon as essential and it was this extra-ordinary fact that first drew my attention to the possible connection of the murderer with the black art.

Further, in the practice of evocation the sacrifice of human victims was a necessary part of the process, and the profanation of the cross and other emblems usually considered sacred was

...the skin of a suicide, nails from a murderer's gallows, candles made from human fat, the head of a black cat...

also enjoined. In this connection it will be well to remember one most extraordinary and unparalleled circumstance in the commission of the Whitechapel murders, and a thing which could not by any possibility have been brought about fortuitously. Leaving out the last murder, committed indoors, which was most probably not committed by the fiend of whom we speak, we find that the sites of the murders, six in number, form a perfect cross. That is to say, a line ruled from No. 3 to No. 6, on a map having the murder sites marked and numbered, passes exactly through Nos. 1 and 2, while the cross arms are accurately formed by a line from No. 4 to 5. The seventh, or Dorset-street murder, does not fall within either of these lines, and there is nothing to connect it with the others except the mutilations. But the mutilations in this latter case were evidently not made by any one having the practical knowledge of the knife and the position of the respective organs which was exhibited in the other six cases, and also in the mutilated trunk found in the new police-buildings, which was probably the first of the series of murders, and was committed somewhere on the lines of the cross, the body being removed at the time. Did the murderer, then, designing to offer the mystic number of seven human sacrifices in the form of a cross – a form

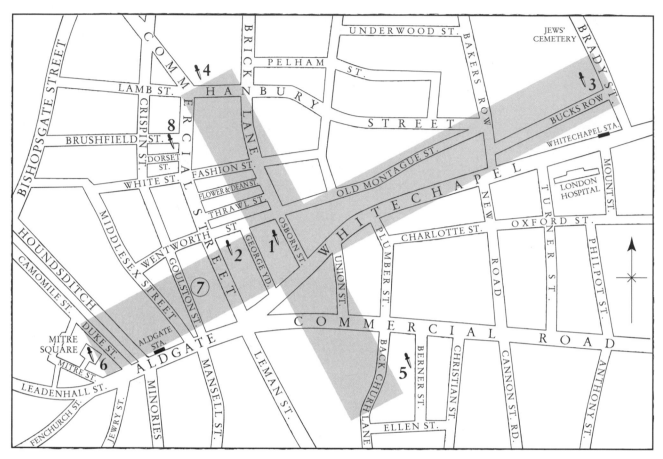

Do the murder sites form a perfect cross? 1. Emma Smith 2. Martha Tabram 3. Polly Nichols 4. Annie Chapman 5. Elizabeth Stride 6. Catherine Eddowes 7. Goulston Street Graffiti 8. Mary Kelly. Note the proximity of Middlesex Street, residence of Joseph Levy, to all the action

which he intended to profane — deliberately pick out beforehand on a map the places in which he would offer them to his infernal deity of murder? If not, surely these six coincidences are the most marvellous event of our time.

To those persons to whom this theory may seem somewhat far-fetched, we would merely remark that the French book referred to was only published a few years ago; that thousands of copies were sold; that societies have been formed for the study and practice of its teachings and philosophy; and, finally, that within the last twelve months an English

edition has been issued. In all things history repeats itself, and the superstitions of yesterday become the creeds of today.'

The Ripper and the Beast

If one man could be said to match the Ripper for notoriety it was the infamous occultist Aleister Crowley. Crowley's reputation for outrageous behaviour led the press to dub him 'the wickedest man in the world'; he enjoyed nothing more than provoking polite society with his salacious stories, one of which concerned the bisexual novelist Mabel Collins, her lesbian lover

Vittoria Cremers, Collins's former lover Robert Donston Stephenson and Jack the Ripper. Crowley's contemporary document reads:

'Some few years before Whitechapel achieved its peculiar notoriety, the white flame of passion which had consumed the fair Mabel [Collins] and her lover, who passed by the name of Captain Donston, had died down; in fact he had become rather more than less of a nuisance; and she was doing everything in her power to get rid of him. Naturally eager to assist in this manoeuvre was her new mistress, a lady passing under the name of Baroness Cremers . . .

[Donston] drifted first into studies medical, and (later) theological. He was a man of extremely aristocratic appearance and demeanour; his manners were polished and his whole behaviour quiet, gentle, and composed; he gave the impression of understanding any possible situation and of ability to master it, but he possessed that indifference to meddling in human affairs which often tempers the activity of people who are conscious of their superiority.

These three people were still living together in Mabel Collins' house in London . . . and for one reason or another [Donston] thought it right to maintain his influence over Mabel Collins . . . and it made her all the more anxious to get rid of him; judging everybody by herself, she was quite sure he would not hesitate to use [her] love-letters in case of definite breach; so, to carry out her scheme, the first procedure must obviously be to obtain possession of the compromising packet and destroy it . . .

One of the relics of his career in the cavalry was a tin uniform case, and this he kept under his bed very firmly secured to the brass frame-work. This, of all his receptacles, was the only one which was always kept locked. From this, Cremers deduced that as likely as not the documents of which she was in search were in the trunk, and she determined to investigate at leisure . . .

Cremers arranged one day for a telegram to be dispatched to Donston, informing him that some friend or near relative had met with a street accident, had been taken to Guy's Hospital, and wanted to see him. Donston immediately started off on this fictitious errand. As he left the house, Mabel laughingly warned him not to get lost and run into Jack the Ripper . . . it may be proper to explain that these events coincided with the Whitechapel murders. On the day of his journey, two or three of them had already been committed – in any case sufficient to start talk and present the murderer with his nick-name. All London was discussing the numerous problems connected with the murders; in particular it seemed to everybody extraordinary that a man for whom the police were looking everywhere could altogether escape notice in view of the nature of the crime. It is hardly necessary to go into the cannibalistic details, but it is quite obvious that a person who is devouring considerable

Aleister Crowley, English writer and magician, was dubbed 'the wickedest man in the world' by the press

chunks of raw flesh, cut from a living body, can hardly do so without copious evidence on his chest.'

At this point Crowley departs from his lurid tale to relate an earlier incident involving the same three characters which had initially aroused the ladies' suspicions.

'One evening, Donston had just come in from the theatre – in those days everyone dressed, whether they liked it or not – and he found the women discussing this point. He gave a slight laugh, went into the passage, and returned in the opera cloak which he had been wearing to the theatre. He turned up the collar and pulled the cape across his shirtfront, made a slight gesture as if to say: "You see how simple it is;" and when a social difficulty presented itself, he remarked lightly: "Of course you cannot have imagined that the man could be a gentleman," and added: "There are plenty going about the East End in evening dress, what with opium smoking and one thing and another" . . .

To return from this long explanatory digression, it was necessary in order to give the fair Cremers time to extricate the uniform case from its complex ropes, the knots being carefully memorised, and to pick the locks.

During this process her mind had been far from at ease; first of all, there seemed to be no weight. Surely a trunk so carefully treasured could not be empty; but if there were a packet of letters more or less loose, there should have been some response to the process of shaking. Her curiosity rose to fever pitch; at last the lock yielded to her persuasive touch; she lifted the lid. The trunk was not empty, but its contents, although few, were striking.

Five white dress ties soaked in blood.'

The magical rites of Jack the Ripper

As a footnote to his article Crowley offered his theory on how the Whitechapel murderer might have escaped detection. It was prompted in part by a speculative piece in the Pall Mall Gazette by Donston, who had hidden behind the pen name Tau Tria Delta.

'After the last of the murders, an article appeared in . . . the Pall Mall Gazette, by Tau Tria Delta, who offered a solution for the motive of the murders. It stated that in one of the grimoires of the Middle Ages, an account was given of a process by which a sorcerer could attain "the supreme black magical power" by following out a course of action identical with that of Jack the Ripper; certain lesser powers were granted to him spontaneously during the course of the proceedings. After the third murder, if memory serves, the assassin obtained on the spot the gift of invisibility, because in the third or fourth murder, a constable on duty saw a man and a woman go into a cul-de-sac. At the end there were the great gates of a factory, but at the sides

The five-pointed star has been adopted as a magic symbol in many different cultures

The number of murders involved in the ceremonies was five, whereas the Whitechapel murders so-called, were seven in number; but two of these were spurious . . . These murders are completely to be distinguished from the five genuine ones, by obvious divergence on technical points.

The place of each murder is important, for it is essential to describe what is called the averse pentagram, that is to say, a star of five points with a single point in the direction of the South Pole.'

From this point Crowley refers to himself in the third person, presumably in an effort to give his theory an air of scientific respectability.

'The investigation has been taken up by Bernard O'Donnell, the crime expert of the Empire News; and he has discovered many interesting details. In the course of conversation with Aleister Crowley this matter came up, and the magician was very impressed with O'Donnell's argument. He suggested an astrological investigation. Was there anything significant about the times of the murders? O'Donnell's investigations had led him to the conclusion that the murderer had attached the greatest importance to accuracy in the time. O'Donnell, accordingly, furnished Crowley with the necessary data, and figures of the heavens were set up . . .

Crowley thought this an excellent opportunity to trace the evil influence of

no doorways or even windows. The constable, becoming suspicious, watched the entry to the gateway, and hearing screams, rushed in. He found the woman, mutilated, but still living; as he ran up, he flashed his bullseye in every direction; and he was absolutely certain that no other person was present. And there was no cover under the archway for so much as a rat.

the planets, looking naturally first of all to Saturn, the great misfortune, then to Mars, the lesser misfortune; but also to Uranus, a planet not known to the ancients, but generally considered of a highly explosive tendency. The result of Crowley's investigations was staggering; there was one constant element in all cases of murder, both of the assassin and the murdered. Saturn, Mars, and Herschel were indeed rightly suspected of doing dirty work at the crossroads, but the one constant factor was a planet which had until that moment been considered, if not actively beneficent, at least perfectly indifferent and harmless – the planet Mercury. Crowley went into this matter very thoroughly and presently it dawned on his rather slow intelligence that after all this was only to be expected; the quality of murder is not primarily malice, greed, or wrath; the one essential condition without which deliberate murder can hardly ever take place, is just this cold-bloodedness, this failure to attribute the supreme value of human life. Armed with these discoveries the horoscopes of the Whitechapel murders shone crystal clear to him. In every case, either Saturn or Mercury were precisely on the Eastern horizon at the moment of the murder (by precisely, one means within a matter of minutes).

Mercury is, of course, the God of Magic, and his averse distorted image the Ape of Thoth, responsible for such evil trickery as is the heart of black magic, while Saturn is not only the cold heartlessness of age, but the magical equivalent of Saturn. He is the old god who was worshipped in the Witches' Sabbath.'

A method to his madness?

It was perhaps inevitable that the Ripper killings would become a fertile ground for conspiracy theorists and their spurious speculations. The royal connection proposed by author Stephen Knight in the 1970s involving Queen Victoria's personal physician Sir William Gull, Prince Albert Victor and the Freemasons captured the public imagination to such an extent that many now believe it to have a basis in fact. Less well known, but equally persistent, is the idea that the victims were ritually slaughtered at predetermined locations to conform to a pattern of occult significance.

The cross

At the time of the killings it was widely believed that the Ripper was a religious fanatic who had set out to rid the streets of prostitutes in a personal crusade against the sin he saw as staining the heart of a Christian capital. An alternative theory, with almost equal support, was the belief that he was a Satanist who killed to obtain specific organs for use in black magic rituals. Whichever was the case, it is argued that he chose specific locations so that they would form a cross, either to scourge the district with the most potent symbol of the Christian faith or to denigrate it.

Such implausible theories are not new, but were given wide publicity at the time as the extract from the *Pall Mall Gazette* dated 1 December 1888 on page 155 reveals. This article is of particular interest because its author, Robert Donston Stephenson, is now considered a prime suspect in the Ripper killings (see also page 123).

When considering D'onston's theory it should be remembered that at the time of its publication Emma Smith and Martha Tabram were thought to have been the first two victims and so when D'onston talks of drawing a line from victims three to six, he is referring to Polly Nichols and Catherine Eddowes. Annie Chapman and Elizabeth Stride are his fourth and fifth victims with Mary Kelly being number seven. The torso he refers to as having been discovered in the foundations of New Scotland Yard (then under construction) has subsequently been shown to have no connection to the Ripper murders, but at the time it was considered part of the series.

Ripperologists Jay Clarke and John Banks recently subjected D'Onston's cross theory to analysis by a respected Canadian statistician and asked him to calculate the probability of finding four randomly positioned bodies in a city which formed a cross. According to the statistician the odds in favour of D'Onston's assertion were one in 15,249,024. But either the professor's basis for the calculation was flawed or Clarke and Banks were highly selective in their interpretation of his findings as mathematician Dan Norder proved quite the opposite in an article for *Ripper Notes* (October 2004), the international journal for Ripper studies. According to Norder, 'When doing calculations of this sort, the size of the number alone in no way proves whether something was random or not. It just proves that there are lots of different possible outcomes.'

And he makes another important point which needs to be borne in mind when considering the conspiracy theories: 'Looking at the map shows that the main roads, although somewhat irregular, mostly form the shape of a cross all by themselves. In other words, most of the features of the patterns people see in the crime scene locations were already present in the layout of the East End before the Ripper killed his first victim.'

It is argued that he chose specific locations so that they would form a cross, either to scourge the district or to denigrate it

The hidden pattern hypothesis

Other symbols and patterns projected onto the murder sites include an arrow whose point is obligingly directed at the Houses of Parliament, a pentagram (a five-pointed star) and a *vesica piscis*, which is a mouth-shaped ellipse, symbolic of the womb. Proponents of the arrow theory exclude the Eddowes murder, which disrupts their pattern, on the grounds that she might have been killed in mistake for Mary Kelly because she used a similar sounding 'street name' – an unlikely scenario in the light of the fact that Eddowes was ten years older and looked nothing like Kelly!

There is another fundamental flaw in the argument of those who see an occult significance where one does not exist and that is that although Catherine Eddowes is listed among the five canonical victims she is unlikely to have been a Ripper victim, and Mary Kelly, whom they discount, was probably his last. Taking Eddowes out of the sequence and adding Kelly disrupts the symmetry and so they are selective with their victims, which undermines their credibility at a stroke.

In their eagerness to uncover a conspiracy or hitherto unknown motive, the advocates of the hidden pattern hypothesis overlook the fact that city maps of the period were notoriously inaccurate; they were intended merely to indicate the relationship of the streets to one another. On all but the official civic engineers' plans, distances were approximate. Consequently one cannot rely on them to prove a correlation between the location of the bodies and the pattern one might wish to superimpose over the area.

Once you start playing 'join the dots' you can make any series of random events and locations assume an unintentional significance provided that you are selective in choosing the pattern you wish them to conform to. Why stop at religious and occult symbols when there are equally good letters that can be formed by connecting the sites? Given time and a considerable degree of latitude, a resourceful conspiracy theorist might be able to form the initials of a member of the monarchy or perhaps even a high-ranking police official. But even if there was an esoteric meaning connecting the location of the murder sites, the mutilations or the timing of the killings, it is ultimately irrelevant as no serial killer merits having his delusions taken seriously. It is what he did and the effect he had on society that is worth considering, not his morbid fantasies.

The man who 'saw' the Ripper

It is not an exaggeration to say that today psychics are consulted on an almost routine basis when the authorities have exhausted all conventional avenues of investigation. But in Victorian England spiritualists, as they were then known, were regarded at best as being a novelty music-hall act or at worst as fraudsters preying on the weak-minded and bereaved. The fact that clairvoyant Robert James Lees had been consulted on several occasions by Queen Victoria did not make him a credible witness as far as Scotland Yard were concerned. When Lees offered his services as a psychic sleuth it is said that they laughed him out of the building. However, if the account published by ex-Scotland Yard officer Edwin T. Woodhall (author of *Secrets of Scotland Yard*) is to be believed, they were soon to regret their rash decision.

'Speculation has always been rife as to Jack the Ripper's identity,' Woodhall began, 'He was never brought to justice but it is a mistake to think that the police did not know who he was. It was proved beyond doubt that he was a physician of the highest standing who lived in a fine house in the West End of London. To most people he was the most refined and gentle of men, both courteous and kind. But he was also an ardent vivisectionist and a cruel sadist who took fierce delight in inflicting pain on helpless creatures.'

According to Woodhall, the identity of this real-life Jekyll and Hyde was revealed by Lees after he had finally convinced the police of the value of his visions.

Visions of murder

The first of the visions had occurred the day after the August Bank Holiday and involved the murder of Martha Tabram. During a trance Lees had 'seen' a man and a woman walking down a 'mean street' into a courtyard and noted the name George Yard Buildings and the time, 12.30, on a nearby clock. The man was dressed in a light tweed suit and carried a dark raincoat. He had a black felt hat pulled down over his eyes and, judging by his steady walk, he was sober, unlike his companion, who staggered under the influence of drink. In the next instant he pressed his hand over the woman's mouth, drew a knife and soundlessly slit her throat. When he had finished inflicting the mutilations he dragged her into a doorway and made his escape, wrapping himself in the raincoat to hide the bloodstains.

Lees was so unsettled by what he had 'seen' and so discouraged by the scepticism with which he had been rebuffed at Scotland Yard that he went abroad to recover, returning shortly after the third murder.

He had hoped that the vision was an isolated occurrence, but one day while travelling on a London omnibus with his wife, Lees was overwhelmed by the same oppressive sensation that had attended his earlier experience. The feeling intensified when a man boarded the bus at Notting Hill wearing the same tweed coat, black felt hat and dark raincoat Lees had seen in the vision. With no word of explanation to his wife, Lees left the bus at Marble Arch to pursue the man he knew to be the Ripper. Lees followed him through Hyde Park, but lost the trail when the suspect caught a hansom cab. Frantic that the murderer might escape, he summoned a policeman and urged him to follow, but the constable

The psychic side of the street: fin-de-siècle London was bustling in the daytime but filled with shadows from the past

refused, offering only to make a note of the incident.

That night Lees was plagued by another terrifying vision and in the morning he went straight to Scotland Yard and urged the detectives in charge of the case to allow him access to the site of the latest murder. According to Woodhall's version of events, they reluctantly agreed and a short time later at Miller's Court, Dorset Street, Lees relived the murder of Mary Kelly.

Lees is vindicated

Once he had recovered sufficiently he began walking westward with the detectives in his wake. Finally he stopped in front of a large town house in the most prosperous part of the West End. Here, Lees insisted, was the home of the Whitechapel murderer. The detectives tried to persuade him that he must be mistaken as it was the home of an eminent physician. But Lees was adamant and to the astonishment of the detectives he described the inside of the house in considerable detail, although he had never been there.

Obliged to pursue the matter, if only to appease Lees and put the matter to rest, the detectives knocked on the door and asked if the master was at home. To their astonishment the interior was exactly as Lees had described it. In making discreet enquiries they learned from the lady of the house that she had always suspected her husband led a double life

and that he enjoyed inflicting pain. The doctor was consequently declared insane and committed to an asylum, but to ensure that his name and reputation were not blackened it was agreed that he should officially be declared dead from heart failure and a mock funeral held so as not to arouse suspicion.

In gratitude for tracking down the Ripper, Lees was reputedly awarded a life pension and sworn to secrecy, a promise he kept until his death in 1931.

The strange psychic visions of Derek Acorah

Psychics fall into two distinct categories. The first are attention-seeking charlatans who go 'fishing' for clues and the second are genuinely gifted individuals who possess an acute sensitivity to residual personal energy. Because of this, they can pick up visual impressions from personal possessions and locations where an earthbound spirit may linger. Celebrated medium Derek Acorah has earned a formidable reputation in England and the USA as a psychic investigator and so was an obvious choice to try his talents at the Whitechapel murder sites.

In April 1999 Acorah was invited by the International Society For Paranormal Research to visit Mitre Square and Bucks Row (now Durward Street) in the company of ISPR parapsychologist Dr Larry Montz and Ripper historian Donald Rumbelow. At the first location the spring sunshine and sounds of the local school children faded, he said, as he tuned into the lingering impressions from more than a hundred years earlier. Through his 'inner eye' he saw the square as it had been on the night of 30 September 1888 and heard the sounds issuing from a nearby public house (since demolished)

A journey into the past

A woman's hoarse laughter rang out and he caught the name 'Catherine'. A moment later she appeared before him, dressed in dark shabby clothes with wisps of grey hair protruding from beneath a greasy bonnet. Acorah was overwhelmed as he shared her sense of dread and inhaled the stench of blood. Recovering his senses, he was drawn to a specific spot which he correctly identified as the place where Catherine Eddowes' body had been found that night. Then he caught another name, 'Elizabeth', as he relived the frenzied attack on Elizabeth Stride, the first of the two victims claimed by the Ripper that evening just a few hundred yards away in Berner Street.

At the next site, Bucks Row, Acorah allowed himself to sink into another light trance in which he 'saw' the mutilated body of the first canonical victim, Polly Nichols, murdered on 31 August 1888. She was stocky and dark-haired, and her clothes were caked with blood. Her face had been slashed and one ear was partially severed. Nearby lay her black straw hat.

When the psychic returned to the present he said he had the impression that the murders were the work of two men. The man responsible for five killings was tall, slim and in his thirties. He had dark facial hair with fringes of grey, high cheekbones and strong crease marks down each side of his face. He was evidently a man of means with possible connections to royalty and carried a pocket watch to which he was constantly referring. The other was a 'copy cat' killer who carried out at least one killing. In both cases the killings were ritualistic rather than sexual or sadistic.

Of course, none of this verifies Acorah's claims to be a genuine clairvoyant (in fact it is an uncharacteristically weak 'performance' by his standards), nor does it reveal details that were not public knowledge, but his assertion that there were two killers is intriguing – if you accept psychic insight as a valid method of investigation.

CHAPTER 6 | THE SCOTLAND YARD FILES

Sir Melville Macnaghten wrote his influential and ultimately highly misleading memorandum on 23 February 1894 to refute newspaper reports that a disturbed young man named Thomas Cutbush had been identified by Scotland Yard as Jack the Ripper. No doubt the press were aroused by the fact that Cutbush had been a medical student and evidently mentally unstable. But as Macnaghten points out, a savage serial killer would be unlikely to be satisfied with prodding young women in the rear with a knife.

'Confidential

The case referred to in the sensational story told in "The Sun" in its issue of 13th inst, & following dates, is that of Thomas Cutbush who was arraigned at the London County Sessions in April 1891 on a charge of maliciously wounding Florence Grace Johnson, and attempting to wound Isabella Fraser Anderson in Kennington. He was found to be insane, and sentenced to be detained during Her Majesty's Pleasure. This Cutbush, who lived with his mother and aunt at 14 Albert Street, Kennington, escaped from the Lambeth Infirmary (after he had been detained only a few hours, as a lunatic) at noon on 5th March 1891. He was rearrested on 9th idem. A few weeks before this, several cases of stabbing, or jabbing, from behind had occurred in the vicinity, and a man named Colicott was arrested, but subsequently discharged owing to faulty identification. The cuts in the girls' dresses made by Colicott were quite different to the cut(s) made by Cutbush (when he wounded Miss Johnson) who was no doubt influenced by a wild desire of morbid imitation. Cutbush's antecedents were enquired into by C. Insp (now Supt.) Chris, by Inspector Hale, and by P.S. McCarthy C.I.D. – (the last named officer had been specially employed in Whitechapel at the time of the murders there) – and it was ascertained that he was born, and had lived, in Kennington all his life. His father died when he was quite young and he was always a "spoilt" child. He had been employed as a clerk and traveller in the Tea trade at the Minories, and subsequently canvassed for a Directory in the East End, during which time he bore a good character. He apparently contracted syphilis about 1888, and, – since that time, – led an idle and useless life. His brain seems to have become affected, and he believed that people were trying to poison him. He wrote to Lord Grimthorpe, and others, – and also to the Treasury, – complaining of Dr Brooks, of Westminster Bridge Road, whom he threatened to shoot for having supplied him with bad medicines. He is said to have studied medical books by day, and to have rambled about at night, returning frequently with his clothes covered with mud; but little reliance could be placed on the statements made by his mother or his aunt, who both appear to have been of a very excitable disposition. It was found impossible to ascertain his movements on the nights of the Whitechapel murders. The knife found on him was bought in Houndsditch about a week before he was detained in the Infirmary. Cutbush was the nephew of the late Supt. Executive.

Now the Whitechapel murderer had 5

Sir Melville Mcnaghten, the Scotland Yard chief, whose report was first made available to the public in 1959

victims – & 5 victims only, – his murders were

(1) 31st August, '88. Mary Ann Nichols – at Buck's Row – who was found with her throat cut – & with (slight) stomach mutilation.

(2) 8th Sept. '88 Annie Chapman – Hanbury St.; – throat cut – stomach & private parts badly mutilated & some of the entrails placed round the neck.

(3) 30th Sept. '88. Elizabeth Stride – Berner's Street – throat cut, but nothing in shape of mutilation attempted, & on same date Catherine Eddowes – Mitre Square, throat cut & very bad

mutilation, both of face and stomach. 9th November. Mary Jane Kelly – Miller's Court, throat cut, and the whole of the body mutilated in the most ghastly manner –

The last murder is the only one that took place in a room, and the murderer must have been at least 2 hours engaged. A photo was taken of the woman, as she was found lying on the bed, without seeing which it is impossible to imagine the awful mutilation.

With regard to the double murder which took place on 30th September, there is no doubt but that the man was disturbed by some Jews who drove up to a Club, (close to which the body of Elizabeth Stride was found) and that he then, "mordum satiatus", went in search of a further victim who he found at Mitre Square.

It will be noted that the fury of the mutilations increased in each case, and, seemingly, the appetite only became sharpened by indulgence. It seems, then, highly improbable that the murderer would have suddenly stopped in November '88, and been content to recommence operations by merely prodding a girl behind some 2 years and 4 months afterwards. A much more rational theory is that the murderer's brain gave way altogether after his awful glut in Miller's Court, and that he

> *A photo was taken of the woman, as she was found lying on the bed... it is impossible to imagine the awful mutilation*

immediately committed suicide, or, as a possible alternative, was found to be so hopelessly mad by his relations, that he was by them confined in some asylum.

No one ever saw the Whitechapel murderer; many homicidal maniacs were suspected, but no shadow of proof could be thrown on any one. I may mention the cases of 3 men, any one of whom would have been more likely than Cutbush to have committed this series of murders:

(1) A Mr M. J. Druitt, said to be a doctor & of good family – who disappeared at the time of the Miller's Court murder, & whose body (which was said to have been upwards of a month in the water) was found in the Thames on 31st December – or about 7 weeks after that murder. He was sexually insane and from private information I have little doubt but that his own family believed him to have been the murderer.

(2) Kosminski – a Polish Jew – & resident in Whitechapel. This man became insane owing to many years' indulgence in solitary vices. He had a great hatred of women, specially of the prostitute class, & had strong homicidal tendencies: he was removed to a lunatic asylum about March 1889. There were many circumstances connected with this man which made him a strong "suspect".

(3) Michael Ostrog, a Russian doctor, and a convict, who was subsequently

detained in a lunatic asylum as a homicidal maniac. This man's antecedents were of the worst possible type, and his whereabouts at the time of the murders could never be ascertained.

And now with regard to a few of the other inaccuracies and misleading statements made by "The Sun". In its issue of 14th February, it is stated that the writer has in his possession a facsimile of the knife with which the murders were committed. This knife (which for some unexplained reason has, for the last 3 years, been kept by Inspector Hale, instead of being sent to Prisoner's Property Store) was traced, and it was found to have been purchased in Houndsditch in February '91 or 2 years and 3 months after the Whitechapel murders ceased!

The statement, too, that Cutbush "spent a portion of the day in making rough drawings of the bodies of women, and of their mutilations" is based solely on the fact that 2 scribble drawings of women in indecent postures were found torn up in Cutbush's room. The head and body of one of these had been cut from some fashion plate, and legs were added to shew a woman's naked thighs and pink stockings.

In the issue of 15th inst. it is said that a light overcoat was among the things found in Cutbush's house, and that a man in a light overcoat was seen talking to a woman at Backchurch Lane whose body with arms attached was found in Pinchin Street. This is hopelessly incorrect! On 10th Sept. '89 the naked body, with arms, of a woman was found wrapped in some sacking under a Railway arch in Pinchin Street: the head

STREET BALLADS

In famous London city in eighteen eighty-eight
Four beastly cruel murders have been done
Some say it was Old Nick himself or else
a Russian Jew
Some say it was a cannibal from the Isle
of Kickaiboo
Some say it must be Bashi-Bazouks
Or else it's the Chinese
Come over to Whitechapel to commit
Such crimes as these.

'As anyone seen him? Can you tell us where he is?
If you meet him, you must take away his knife
Then give him to the women, they'll spoil his
pretty fiz,
And I wouldn't give him tuppence for his life.

Now at night when you're undressed and about to go
to rest
Just see that he ain't underneath the bed
If he is you mustn't shout but politely drag
him out
And with your poker tap him on the head

Eight little whores, with no hope of heaven,
Gladstone may save one, then there'll be seven.
Seven little whores beggin' for a shilling,
One stays in Henage Court, then there's
a killing.
Six little whores, glad to be alive,
One sidles up to Jack, then there are five.
Four and whore rhyme aright,
So do three and me,
I'll set the town alight
Ere there are two.
Two little whores, shivering with fright,
Seek a cosy doorway in the middle of the night.
Jack's knife flashes, then there's but one,
And the last one's the ripest for
Jack's idea of fun.

A knife reputedly
used by Jack
the Ripper

A knife reputedly
used by Jack
the Ripper

and legs were never found nor was the woman ever identified. She had been killed at least 24 hours before the remains which had seemingly been brought from a distance, were discovered. The stomach was split up by a cut, and the head and legs had been severed in a manner identical with that of the woman whose remains were discovered in the Thames, in Battersea Park, and on the Chelsea Embankment on the 4th June of the same year; and these murders had no connection whatever with the Whitechapel horrors. The Rainham mystery in 1887 and the Whitehall mystery (when portions of a woman's body were found under what is now New Scotland Yard) in 1888 were of a similar type to the Thames and Pinchin Street crimes.

It is perfectly untrue to say that Cutbush stabbed 6 girls behind. This is confounding his case with that of Colicott. The theory that the Whitechapel murderer was left-handed, or, at any rate, "ambidexter", had its origin in the remark made by a doctor who examined the corpse of one of the earliest victims; other doctors did not agree with him.

With regard to the 4 additional murders ascribed by the writer in the Sun to the Whitechapel fiend:

(1) The body of Martha Tabram, a prostitute, was found on a common staircase in George Yard buildings on 7th August 1888; the body had been repeatedly pierced, probably with a bayonet. This woman had, with a fellow prostitute, been in company of 2 soldiers in the early part of the evening: these men were arrested, but the second prostitute failed, or refused, to identify, and the soldiers were eventually discharged.

(2) Alice McKenzie was found with her throat cut (or rather stabbed) in Castle Alley on 17th July 1889; no evidence was forthcoming and no arrests were made in connection with this case. The stab in the throat was of the same nature as in the case of the murder of

(3) Frances Coles in Swallow Gardens, on 13th February 1891 – for which Thomas Sadler, a fireman, was arrested,

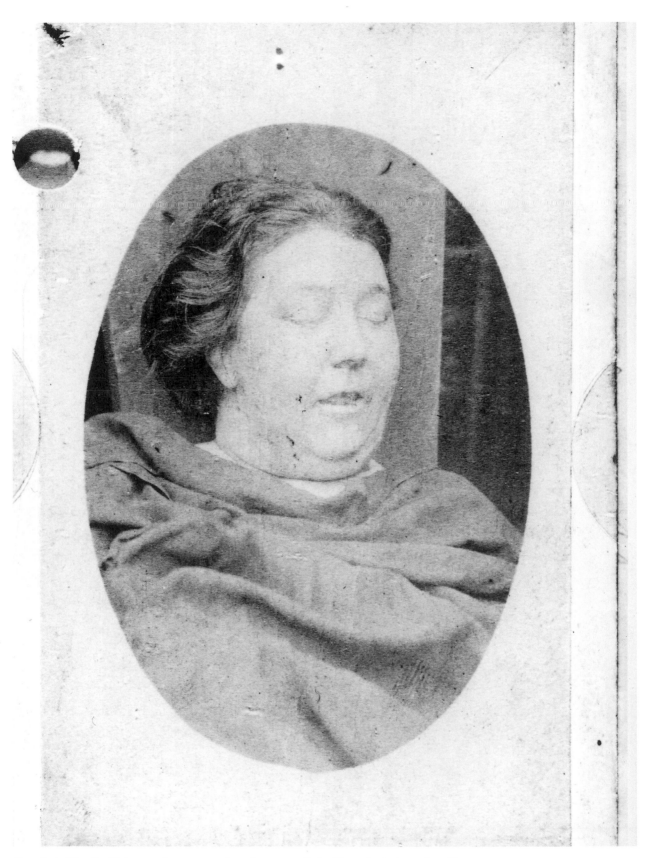

Prostitute Martha Tabram who may not have been one of the Ripper's victims after all

and, after several remands, discharged. It was ascertained at the time that Sadler had sailed for the Baltic on 19th July '89 and was in Whitechapel on the night of 17th idem. He was a man of ungovernable temper and entirely addicted to drink, and the company of the lowest prostitutes.
(4) The case of the unidentified woman whose trunk was found in Pinchin Street: on 10th September 1889 – which has already been dealt with.
M.S. Macnaghten
23rd February 1894'

The missing Ripper files

When the official police files were transferred from Scotland Yard to the Public Record Office in the 1980s several of the files itemized on the inventory were found to be missing. Fortunately, extensive notes had been made by various researchers shortly before they disappeared, preserving the names of a number of significant suspects who would otherwise have been overlooked.

A soldier suspected

One of the most promising is a report from the police at Rotherham dated 5 October, concerning a soldier with a violent hatred of women. Their informant, James Oliver, a former member of the 5th Lancers, was 'firmly persuaded in his own mind' that one of his former comrades was responsible for the Whitechapel murders.

The accused, Richard Austen, had been a sailor and was about 40 years old when the report was written. From the description of his appearance and behaviour, he seems a likely candidate for questioning, but the authorities were never able to trace him.

Oliver's statement described him as:

'. . . 5ft 8in, an extremely powerful and active man, but by no means heavy or stout. Hair and eyes light, had in service a very long fair moustache, may have grown heavy whiskers and beard. His face was fresh, hard and healthy looking. He had a small piece bitten off the end of his nose. Although not mad, he was not right in his mind, "he was too sharp to be right" . . . He used to sometimes brag of what he had done previously to enlisting in the way of violence . . . While in the regiment he was never known to go with women and when his comrades used to talk about them in the barrack room he used to grind his teeth – he was in fact a perfect woman hater. He used to say if he had his will he would kill every whore and cut her inside out, that when he left the regiment there would be nothing before him but the gallows . . . Probably he would always be respectably dressed but more often the description of a sailor than a soldier.'

Oliver presumed he would be working at London Docks or on board ship and that he may have committed the murders shortly before embarking on a

Passport to freedom: amid the hustle and bustle of London's docks, the Ripper could easily have slipped away

new voyage – which would account for the long gaps between murders. Oliver was convinced that if Austen could be traced his return to port would tally with the dates of the murders. 'He always had revenge brooding on his mind,' he said.

Oliver offered to identify Austen from a regimental photograph if one could be supplied and to look at the 'Dear Boss' letters to see if the handwriting matched that of his former comrade. However, no photograph could be found, but when facsimiles of the letters were sent down from London Oliver stated that the writing was very similar to Austen's. Austen was never traced and the police had no choice but to abandon that line of enquiry.

Dr Winslow's accusation

The following press cutting from the *New York Herald* dated September 1889 was evidently considered worthy of serious investigation as it had originally been preserved in the now missing police files by Chief Inspector Swanson, who subsequently interviewed Dr Forbes Winslow in an attempt to verify the story. Fortunately someone had the presence of mind to photocopy it before both the press cutting and the file containing Swanson's notes went missing in the 1970s.

'The Whitechapel Murders
A report having been current that a man

has been found who is quite convinced that "Jack the Ripper" occupied rooms in his house, and that he had communicated his suspicions in the first instance to Dr Forbes Winslow, together with detailed particulars, a reporter had an interview with the doctor yesterday afternoon on the subject.

"Here are Jack the Ripper's boots," said the doctor, at the same time taking a large pair of boots out from under his table. *"The tops of these boots are made of ordinary cloth material, while the soles are made of indiarubber. The tops have great bloodstains on them."*

The reporter put the boots on and found they were completely noiseless. Besides these noiseless coverings the doctor says he has the Ripper's ordinary walking boots, which are very dirty, and the man's coat which is also bloodstained.

Proceeding, the doctor said that on the morning of Aug. 30 a woman with whom he was in communication was spoken to by a man in Worship Street, Finsbury. He asked her to come down a certain court with him, offering her £1. This she refused and he then doubled the amount, which she also declined. He next asked her where the court led to and shortly afterwards left. She told some neighbours and the party followed the man for some distance. Apparently, he did not know that he was being followed, but when he and the party had reached the open street he turned round, raised his hat, and with an air of bravado said: "I know what you have been doing; Good morning." The woman then watched the man [go] into a certain house, the situation of which the doctor would not describe. She previously noticed the man because of his strange manner, and on the morning on which the woman Mackenzie was murdered (July 17th) she saw him washing his hands in the yard of the house referred to. He was in his shirt-sleeves at the time, and had a very peculiar look upon his face. This was about four o'clock in the morning.

The doctor said he was now waiting for a certain telegram, which was the only obstacle to his effecting the man's arrest. The supposed assassin lived with a friend of Dr Forbes Winslow, and this gentleman himself told the doctor that he had noticed the man's strange behaviour. He would at times sit down and write 50 or 60 sheets of manuscript about low women, for whom he professed to have great hatred. Shortly before the body was found in Pinchin Street last week the man disappeared, leaving behind him the articles already mentioned, together with a packet of manuscript, which the doctor said was in exactly the same handwriting as the Jack the Ripper letters which were sent to the police. He stated previously that he was going abroad, but a very few days before the body was discovered (Sept. 10) he was seen in the neighbourhood of Pinchin

He could give a reason for the head and legs being missing. The man cut the body up and then commenced to burn it

Street. The doctor is certain that this man is the Whitechapel murderer, and says that two days at the utmost will see him in custody.

He could give a reason for the head and legs of the last murdered woman being missing. The man, he thinks, cut the body up, and then commenced to burn it. He had consumed the head and legs when his fit of the terrible mania passed, and he was horrified to find what he had done. "I know for a fact", said the doctor, "that this man is suffering from a violent form of religious mania, which attacks him and passes off at intervals. I am certain that there is another man in it besides the one I am after, but my reasons for that I cannot state."

Chief Inspector Swanson wasted no time in interviewing Dr Winslow and discovered the identity of the man with the religious mania. He was named as Mr Bell Smith, a Canadian who had been lodging with Mr and Mrs Callaghan of Victoria Park, who were friends of Dr Winslow. The Callaghans had become suspicious of their lodger after he had stayed out until 4am on 7 August, the night of Martha Tabram's murder. Later that day they discovered bloodstains on his bedclothes and noted that he had soaked his shirts in his room, presumably in an attempt to eradicate incriminating stains. The Callaghans regarded their eccentric guest as 'a lunatic with delusions regarding women of the streets', especially those in the East End. The Callaghans confirmed that their lodger's handwriting was an exact match for the Ripper letters which had been widely circulated and published in the press. During his interview with Dr Winslow, Swanson obtained a description of Bell Smith from a letter written by Mr Callaghan to the doctor.

'He is about 5ft 10in in height . . . hair dark, complexion the same, moustache and beard closely cut giving the idea of being unshaven . . . he appeared well conducted, was well dressed and resembled a foreigner, speaking several languages. [He] entertains strong religious delusions about women, and stated that he had done some wonderful operations. His manner and habits were peculiar. Without doubt this man is the perpetrator of these crimes.'

Incredibly, no further information is known about this promising line of inquiry and the trail ends with Swanson's summation of the information received from Callaghan and a note regarding the fact that Inspector Abberline has no record of Dr Winslow's accusation.

The police files

During the investigation police officials were discouraged from giving interviews to the press, but after the Ripper files were closed in 1892 various officers published their memoirs and talked openly to journalists of their suspicions regarding the known suspects.

Metropolitan Police Inspector Frederick Abberline

In 1903 Abberline admitted that 'Scotland Yard is really no wiser on the subject than it was fifteen years ago'. But the same year he reputedly told the *Pall Mall Gazette* that he personally had suspected convicted murderer Severin Klosowski (alias George Chapman) of being the Ripper: 'I cannot help feeling that this was the man we struggled so hard to capture fifteen years ago.' In a letter to Sir Melville Macnaghten written around the same time, he remarked, 'I have been so struck with the remarkable coincidences in the two series of murders, that I have not been able to think of anything else for several days past.' He noted the salient fact that his suspect 'arrived in London shortly before the murders began, and then they stopped after he went to America. He had studied medicine and surgery in Russia, and the series of murders was the work of an expert surgeon.' He felt it pertinent to add that Klosowski was known to have attacked his own wife with a long-bladed knife after they had emigrated to the USA.

In another interview he dismissed the rumour that Kosminski had been

Frederick Abberline

asserted that 'in saying that he was a Polish Jew I am merely stating a definitely ascertained fact', adding, 'One did not need to be a Sherlock Holmes to discover that the criminal was a sexual maniac of a virulent type; that he was living in the immediate vicinity of the scenes of the murders, and that if he was not living absolutely alone, his people knew of his guilt and refused to give him up to justice . . . I will only add that when the individual whom we suspected was caged in an asylum, the only person who had ever had a good view of the murderer at once identified him, but when he learned that the suspect was a fellow Jew, he declined to swear to him.'

It is understood that the suspect to whom he is referring is Kosminski and that the reluctant witness was either Schwartz or Lawende.

identified as the perpetrator, saying, 'It has been stated in several quarters that "Jack the Ripper" was a man who died in a lunatic asylum a few years ago, but there is nothing at all of a tangible nature to support such a theory.' He was equally dismissive of the case against Druitt. 'Soon after the last murder in Whitechapel the body of a young doctor was found in the Thames, but there is absolutely nothing beyond the fact that he was found at the time to incriminate him.'

Sir Robert Anderson

In his autobiography, *The Lighter Side of My Official Life*, Anderson, who was Assistant Commissioner of the CID at the time of the murders, confidently

Donald Swanson, Chief Inspector, CID, Scotland Yard

Swanson later confirmed that the suspect Anderson referred to 'was sent to Stepney Workhouse and then to Colney Hatch and died shortly afterwards', adding, 'Kosminski was the suspect.' But he does not say if he believes that Kosminski was the Ripper, only that he was a suspect.

Chief Inspector John George Littlechild

In 1913 Littlechild wrote privately to journalist George Sims revealing that a substantial dossier had been compiled on a dubious character by the name of Dr Francis Tumblety (see page 137) who remained 'a very likely suspect', but the file has mysteriously vanished from the archives at Scotland Yard.

He concluded the letter by saying that Sir Robert Anderson only 'thought he knew' who the killer was, which suggests that no one actively engaged on the case knew with any certainty.

Assistant Chief Commissioner Sir Melville Macnaghten

Although Macnaghten did not arrive at the Metropolitan Police until June 1889 he familiarized himself with the details of the case and identified Druitt, Ostrog and Kosminski as likely suspects. In the Aberconway version of his famous memorandum he went further, expressing his preference for Druitt. In his memoirs *Days of My Years*, he speculated that 'the Whitechapel murderer in all probability put an end to himself soon after the Dorset Street affair in November 1888, certain facts, pointing to this conclusion, were not in the possession of the police till some years after I became a detective officer.'

Inspector of Prisons Major Arthur Griffiths

In his official capacity Griffiths was in the habit of visiting Scotland Yard and sitting in on discussions between Macnaghten, Anderson and Littlechild, which led him to claim that he was privy to inside information on the Ripper investigation. In *Mysteries of Police and Crime* he confided, 'The general public may think that the identity of Jack the Ripper was never revealed. So far as actual knowledge goes, this is undoubtedly true. But the police, after the last murder, had brought their investigations to the point of strongly suspecting several persons, all of them known to be homicidal lunatics, and against three of these they held very plausible and reasonable grounds of suspicion . . . Concerning two of them the case was weak, although it was based on certain colourable facts. One was a Polish Jew, a known lunatic, who was at large in the district of Whitechapel at the time of the murders, and who, having afterwards developed homicidal tendencies, was confined to an asylum.' This is a clear reference to Kosminski.

Assistant Commissioner James Monro

Monro was not given to speculation. He prided himself on acting on the facts alone, but was so certain that he knew the identity of the Whitechapel murderer that he told his grandson, 'The Ripper was never caught. But he should have been.' It is believed that he had a private file that he left to his eldest son Charles, who in turn shared the contents with his younger brother, Douglas, who described the dossier as 'a very hot potato'. Douglas advised his brother to burn it and to forget what he had read. Unfortunately, Charles did so, so we have no way of corroborating the story.

James Monro, Commissioner of the Metropolitan Police 1888–90, prided himself on acting on the facts alone

Inspector Edmund Reid

Reid, who took charge of the initial investigation after the murder of Martha Tabram, maintained that there were nine victims, the last being Francis Coles. In 1912 he gave his verdict on the case to *Lloyd's Weekly News*, in which he said, 'It still amuses me to read the writings of such men as Dr Anderson, Dr Forbes Winslow, Major Arthur Griffiths, and many others, all holding different theories, but all of them wrong . . . the perpetrator of the crimes was a man who was in the habit of using a certain public-house.' Reid did not have a specific individual in mind, but he had formed an opinion of the type of man who when drunk would lead his drinking companion into a dark corner then 'attack her with the knife and cut her up. Having satisfied his maniacal blood-lust he would go away home, and the next day know nothing about it'. It is thought that he based this belief on a sighting by a witness who had reported seeing a suspicious man with a knife in a public house, but there were so many reports of a similar nature that identification would have proven impractical.

Chief Superintendent Sir Henry Smith

In 1910 Sir Henry Smith, Chief Superintendent of the City of London Police, published his memoirs *From Constable to Commissioner*, in which he claimed that he had a serious contender for the Ripper murders in mind at the time of the Eddowes killing which no other officer had known about. 'He had been a medical student . . . He had been in a lunatic asylum; he spent all his time with women of loose character, whom he bilked by giving them polished farthings instead of sovereigns. I thought he was likely to be in Rupert

Street, Haymarket, so I sent up two men and there he was . . . polished farthings and all, he proved an alibi without a shadow of a doubt.'

With that lead having proven a dead end, he was forced to admit that 'Jack the Ripper beat me and every other police officer in London . . . I have no more idea now where he lived than I had twenty years ago.'

City of London Police Officer Robert Sagar

Sagar was adamant that 'We had good reason to suspect a man who worked in Butcher's Row, Aldgate . . . There was no doubt that this man was insane, and after a time his friends thought it advisable to have him removed to a private asylum. After he was removed there were no more Ripper atrocities.'

The Ripper in the USA

Festering in the shadow of the Brooklyn Bridge on the dockside of lower Manhattan in the spring of 1891 were huddled rows of squalid flophouses to rival those in London's East End. The patrons too were cut from the same threadbare cloth as their English counterparts. In the squalid compartments of the East River Hotel sailors and dockside labourers could bed down in the company of cut-throats, petty criminals and drug addicts for the princely sum of 25 cents a night. Room service was extra – for a few dollars a prostitute could be persuaded to turn a blind eye to the cockroaches and act as if the rough pawing hands of a stranger were a lover's caress. But some of the customers liked to play rough and on the morning of 24 April the desk clerk staggered from Room 31, shaken to the core by what he had just seen. A naked woman lay on the bed, a deep wound extending from the lower abdomen to the breast. She had been strangled then disembowelled and her entrails strewn over the bed. When the police arrived they discovered two deep wounds in her back in the form of a cross. There were rumours that certain organs had been removed. The similarity with the Whitechapel murders was self-evident and quickly seized upon by the newspapers.

'The points of similarity between this crime and those attributed to "Jack the Ripper" are numerous . . . The murdered woman belonged to the lowest class of fallen women from whom "Jack the Ripper" always selected his victims . . . The same horrible act of disembowelment and mutilation which distinguished the Whitechapel atrocities was performed upon this unfortunate hag . . . There was the same abstraction or attempted abstraction of certain organs. The instrument used – a big bladed knife – is similar to the weapon used by the Whitechapel fiend . . . The district in which the murder was committed corresponds . . . to the Whitechapel district of London, especially in respect to the character of many of its inhabitants.'

Talk of the taverns: everyone had their own theory as to who the Ripper was but the mystery persists to this day

Several boasted sources inside the New York police, who confided their fears that the Ripper had fled England and was now loose in the Lower East Side.

Eyewitness account

A preliminary investigation retraced the victim's last known movements. Somewhere between 10.30 and 11.45pm on 23 April she had asked for a room for herself and her companion, a man about 30 years old, 172cm (5ft 8in) in height with brown hair, a brown moustache and a prominent nose. He was wearing a Derby hat and a cutaway coat. He was sullen and silent for the most part, but when he spoke he betrayed a distinct accent, although the main witness, a prostitute named Mrs Miniter, could not recognize from which country he originated.

There was no doubt concerning the victim's identity, however. Her name was Carrie Brown, a 60-year-old widow of a wealthy sea captain and mother of three children who had succumbed to prostitution after falling foul of the demon drink. But in her younger days she had been an actress of some repute and was still given to quoting verse which had led to her being given the nickname 'Old Shakespeare'.

Within three days Inspector Byrnes announced that he had a material witness, an Algerian known locally as 'Frenchy', and was now looking for his cousin who was known by the same soubriquet in connection with the killing. But shortly afterwards, Byrnes surprised both his colleagues and journalists by denying that he had named the Algerian as a suspect. The turnaround baffled reporters, who delighted in reminding their readers that it was Byrnes who had once boasted that he would not have allowed a serial killer to run rings around his men as the London police had done.

Inspector Byrnes' mistake

A few days later Byrnes made another contradictory claim. He now identified the prime suspect as Frenchy No. 1, the man he had been holding as a material witness, whose real name was Ameer Ben Ali.

Frustrated journalists quickly became highly critical of the investigation and demanded, 'Why was it that intelligent reporters did not see the bloody tracks leading across the hall from Room No. 31, the woman's room, to Room No. 33, Frenchy's room, or at least the marks of their erasure? And how was it that they had failed to notice that Room No. 33 had the appearance of a slaughterhouse, as Mr Byrnes says it had? In the opinion of the general public Inspector Byrnes must look a good deal further before he finds the real Jack the Ripper. Sympathy is entirely with Frenchy, and there is a general belief in his innocence. Byrnes must soon admit himself as badly baffled and as much at sea as was Scotland Yard during and after the London butcheries.'

A horse-drawn carriage trundles by in the shadow of the Brooklyn Bridge. Could this have been the Ripper's new haunt?

Others hinted at the real motive behind the embarrassing *volte face*: 'It is charged by the enemies of the Inspector that he is really prosecuting Frenchy to make good his word that a Jack the Ripper could not live here two days in safety.'

During the trial serious doubts were raised regarding Ali's guilt. Reporters who had been on the scene the morning of the murder contradicted the official police version of events while police officers gave conflicting statements. Then it emerged that Ali had not occupied the room to which the mysterious blood trail had led, but incredibly the jury found him guilty nevertheless. He was to spend 11 long years in prison before a concerted press campaign forced the authorities to

The Lower East Side, New York, where newcomers could mix in with the crowd

acknowledge serious misgivings regarding the validity of the evidence and order his release.

A credible suspect

Meanwhile Frenchy No. 2 had been traced and questioned and his connection with the Whitechapel murders revealed by the New York daily *The World*:

'There is a man named "Frenchy" who answers the description of Frenchy No. 2, and who was arrested in London about a year and a half ago in connection with the Whitechapel murders . . . During the past two or three years this man has been crossing back and forth between this country and England on the freight steamers that carry cattle. He is noted for his strength

ON THE TRACK

The summer had come in September at last,
And the pantomime season was coming on fast,
When a score of detectives arrived from the Yard
To untangle a skein which was not very hard.
They looked very wise, and they started a clue;
They twiddled their thumbs as the best thing to do.
They said, "By this murder we're taken aback,
But we're now, we believe, on the murderer's track."
They scattered themselves o'er the face of the land –
A gallant, devoted, intelligent band –
They arrested their suspects north, east, south, and west;
From inspector to sergeant each man did his best.
They took up a bishop, they took up a Bung,
They arrested the old, they arrested the young;
They ran in Bill, Thomas, and Harry and Jack,
Yet still they remained on the murderer's track.
The years passed away and the century waned,
A mystery still the big murder remained.

It puzzled the Bar and it puzzled the Bench,
It puzzled policemen, Dutch, German, and French;
But 'twas clear as a pikestaff to all London 'tecs,
Who to see through a wall didn't want to wear specs.
In reply to the sneer and the snarl and the snack
They exclaimed, "We are still on the murderer's track."
They remained on his track till they died of old age,
And the story was blotted from history's page;
But they died like detectives convinced that the crime
They'd have traced to its source if they'd only had time.
They made a good end, and they turned to the wall
To answer the Great First Commissioner's call;
And they sighed as their breathing grew suddenly slack –
"We believe we are now on the murderer's track."

(George Sims)

and physical prowess . . . The sailors on the cattle ships tell horrible stories of his cruelty to the dumb brutes in his care. When one of these animals would break a leg or receive some injury that necessitated its slaughter, "Frenchy", they say, would take apparent delight in carving it up alive while the sailors looked on. No one dared oppose him, his temper was so bad. When he was arrested on suspicion that he was "Jack the Ripper" he knocked down the officer who tackled him and made things very lively for half a dozen men before they got him under control.'

But just when it appeared that the American authorities had finally collared Jack the Ripper the suspect was released, despite having been positively identified as Carrie Brown's sullen and silent companion by Mary Miniter. It appears that Inspector Byrnes had lost faith in her reliability after having learned that she was a dope addict.

The reporters, however, scented a scoop and were not so easily put off. They traced Frenchy No. 2 to a lodging house and even managed to persuade him to give them an interview. Could this be the one and only time we hear the voice of Jack the Ripper?

'The night of the East River murder I passed in this lodging house . . .' he began. 'My name is Arbie La Bruckman, but I am commonly called John Francis. I was born in Morocco 29 years ago. I arrived here on the steamer *Spain* April 10 from London.'

In reply to a question concerning his

arrest in London La Bruckman answered, 'About 11 o'clock one night a little after Christmas, 1889, I was walking along the street. I carried a small satchel. I was bound for Hull, England, where I was to take another ship. Before I reached the depot, I was arrested and taken to London Headquarters. I was locked up for a month, placed on trial and duly acquitted. After my discharge the Government gave me £100 and a suit of clothes for the inconvenience I had suffered.'

This was contradicted by a subsequent news item which stated that La Bruckman had been in custody for a month on suspicion of being the Ripper and that he was later discharged. There had been no trial. If there had been, all England would have read about it.

Could it have been La Bruckman?

This may be the source of the story published after the murder of Frances Coles in February 1891. 'A policeman who saw the unfortunate woman a short time before the murder said that she was talking to a man who looked like a sailor. The police searched all the cattle ships but found no reason to arrest anyone. Late in the evening, a man was arrested on the docks and locked up on suspicion.'

Although there may not have been sufficient physical evidence to arrest La Bruckman, it is known that the company he worked for, National Line,

had cattle boats in dock at London ports on dates coinciding with the Whitechapel murders.

But the suspicion that La Bruckman knew more about the Carrie Brown murder than he admitted persisted. Further investigations by the tenacious journalists uncovered the following story.

The clerk at the Glenmore Hotel, near the murder scene, remembered being accosted by a man answering La Bruckman's description on the night of the murder. The man, who was in an agitated state, had blood on his hands, his shirtfront and his sleeves. When the clerk refused to give him a room for the night, he asked if he could use the rest room in the lobby to clean himself up, but again the clerk refused. Had Inspector Byrnes pursued this line of inquiry he might have cleared up both the Carrie Brown murder and the mystery of Jack the Ripper, but for reasons known only to himself he chose to prosecute Ali the Algerian and allow La Bruckman to slip through his fingers.

Byrnes' complacency should have been shaken by the discovery of another mutilated corpse just a month after Ali's conviction, but perhaps he did not relish having his assumptions questioned. The *Morning Journal* had no such reservations. 'Is It Jack's Work?' asked their headline the morning after the body of a 45-year-old prostitute had been fished out of the East River. It is a question that remains tantalizingly unanswered to this day.

When conducting a murder investigation, it is common practice to begin with a thorough examination of the crime scene and a re-assessment of the trace evidence, the victim's injuries and the witness statements before considering a possible motive and evaluating the key suspects. The procedure has changed little in over a century and is the same whether it is a current inquiry or a cold case. But in regard to the Whitechapel murders many amateur investigators continue to ignore the basic rules of detection. In their eagerness to prove their own pet theory, they turn the spotlight on their chosen suspect and in a sense 'fit him up' to take the fall instead of allowing the trail of evidence to lead wherever it takes them. This is the same approach favoured by the conspiracy theorists whose personal conviction invariably leads to the construction of an elaborate fantasy based on the selective use of the few facts which happen to support their alternative reality.

The truth of the matter is that, if we want to identify the Whitechapel murderer, we need to scrutinize the facts objectively and resist the temptation to speculate. We must be prepared to eliminate suspects who do not conform to the eyewitness descriptions and trust in the unerringly accurate psychological profiles provided by both Dr Bond, the forensic scientist, and modern FBI profilers, no matter how keen we might be on unmasking our preferred candidate for the notorious murders.

Identifying the victims

But first there is the nagging question of which victims are to be attributed to the Ripper and which to random street violence.

There is every reason to suspect that the unprovoked attack on 38-year-old Annie Millwood on 25 February 1888 by a man armed with a clasp knife may have been a faltering first step on the Ripper's road to infamy. Annie was assaulted in White's Row, just a few minutes' walk from George Yard where Martha Tabram was murdered later that year at 5pm when darkness contrived to screen the stranger's face. Annie was stabbed repeatedly in the legs and abdomen and, although she recovered after three weeks in the Whitechapel Workhouse Infirmary, she died on 31 March from natural causes, no doubt weakened by her injuries.

The second attack occurred shortly after midnight on 27 March after 39-year-old Ada Wilson answered her front door and was set upon by a man who demanded money. When she refused he stabbed her twice in the neck and would certainly have inflicted a fatal wound had he not been frightened off by her screams for help. Ada described her assailant as being aged about 30, 167cm (5ft 6in) tall with a sunburnt complexion and a fair moustache. He wore light trousers, a dark coat and a wideawake hat. Curiously, neither woman has even been considered as a possible Ripper victim, yet they cannot be excluded simply because the murder of the first 'official' victim, Polly Nichols, was still several months away.

Some historians are keen to keep Emma Smith in contention for victim number one, but if she was telling the truth, and there is no reason to doubt her story, she was attacked by a group of roughs and she can therefore be eliminated from the list.

At the time Martha Tabram was believed to be the second victim and it is true that she suffered a frenzied, motiveless assault, but the police surgeon was certain that a bayonet had made the fatal wound (the others having been inflicted with a pen knife), and a local constable had talked with a soldier near the scene who claimed to have been waiting for his comrade who had 'gone off with a woman'. For these reasons Tabram could be excluded as it seems extremely unlikely that she was attacked by a man with a bayonet after the soldier had finished his business with her, although we will never know for certain what took place that night.

The five canonical victims

This leaves what are commonly known as the five canonical victims – Nichols, Eddowes, Stride, Chapman and Kelly. Of these Stride is doubtful as she was murdered by a single knife wound to the throat and was not mutilated. Even allowing for the possibility that the murderer might have been interrupted, it is significant that her throat was apparently cut from right to left, rather than left to right as the others had been, and that Dr Phillips, the police surgeon, testified that there were

distinct differences between her murder and that of the other women. It has to be said, though, that Dr Blackwell disagreed with Dr Bond, contending that it was indeed the work of the same killer, the wound being inflicted left to right, just less forcibly.

But there are two aspects which weigh heavily against Stride being a Ripper victim. The first is that an eyewitness, Israel Schwartz, testified that he saw Stride being assaulted by a man at the spot where she was found just 15 minutes later and from his description it appeared to be a quarrel between a ruffian and his woman or a prostitute and her client which ended with her having her throat cut once Schwartz was out of sight. If so, the killer would have no reason to murder and mutilate a second woman only an hour later. Secondly, if this was the man who killed Stride why did he walk back to Whitechapel after killing Eddowes with the bloody knife and the fragment of her apron in his hand when he must have known that the police were swarming all over the area in the wake of the first murder? The two incidents are surely unrelated.

Unless there were two men – the Ripper and an accomplice who acted as a lookout. Schwartz made a statement to the police in which he described being chased by a second man who was standing on the opposite side of the road to the ruffian who had knocked the woman to the ground. If this second man acted as a lookout it would explain how the Ripper was able to evade arrest. But serial killers rarely work as a team and if these two had done so, what would have driven them to share such a terrible secret? Could they have been brothers? Or ex-army comrades (one armed with a bayonet and one with a short-bladed knife perhaps)? Did they have a score to settle with prostitutes for having given them venereal disease, or were they simply on a crusade to cleanse the streets? It is an intriguing theory, but the lone killer is still the more likely scenario. That said, there is a marked similarity between the ruffian Schwartz describes seeing in Berner Street and the 'rough and shabby' individual seen by Lawende near Mitre Square.

How the Ripper killed his victims

By examining the original post-mortem reports and the testimony given by the police surgeons at the various inquests, it is possible to learn

Crime scene sketch of a Ripper victim

how the Ripper subdued and murdered his victims.

Several historians have suggested that the lack of blood at the crime scenes could be due to the victims having been murdered elsewhere, perhaps even in a closed carriage, and their bodies transported to the location where they were discovered. But the evidence suggests otherwise. Four of the five canonical victims were found on their backs, the blood pooled around them and soaked into the back of their clothes, revealing that they had been attacked from the front. It appears that he took hold of them by the throat and throttled them while they were occupied raising their skirts. Then he lowered them to the ground (as evident from the lack of bruising to the back of the head) with their heads to his left and slit their throats from left to right down to the spinal column, which would have directed any arterial spray from the carotid artery away from him. It is thought that he then pushed their legs up and apart so he could kneel between their knees to carry out the mutilations.

Several of the women had notable bruising around the neck, discoloured faces and swollen tongues, indicating that they had been strangled, which would account for the fact that no one heard any cries for help. This being the case, their hearts would have stopped, which would account for the comparatively small amount of blood at the scene, most of it spilling from the neck wound. The murderer could then have passed through the streets in the early hours of the morning without attracting attention as he would have not have had any sizable amount of blood on his clothes.

The significance of the mutilations

A close examination of the autopsy reports reveals that there is no evidence to support the widely held belief that the murders were the work of a surgeon. This rumour originated with the coroner Wynne Baxter, a notoriously opinionated minor public official who relished his new role as medical expert for which he was clearly unqualified. Although the police surgeons were not always in agreement, there was a consensus that the murderer demonstrated a degree of skill with a knife, but no more so than a butcher or medical student might possess.

The injuries to Polly Nichols showed no medical knowledge or skill whatever. Her throat had been severed down to the vertebrae in two places, suggesting that her murderer might have been trying to decapitate her, but the other wounds to her abdomen appeared to be random and to no particular purpose, which suggests a disorganized state of mind. These incisions, which were not aimed at any specific organ, had been inflicted with considerable force using a moderately sharp, long-bladed knife by a right-handed assailant.

Neither were there ritualistic elements in the murder of Annie Chapman. The placing of the intestines over both her shoulders was done simply to give the killer access to her viscera. As Krafft-Ebbing's study *Psychopathia Sexualis* has shown, it is a compulsive disorder of a certain type of sexual killer to wallow in the guts of their victims.

Had the Ripper been a surgeon or pathologist, he would have had ample opportunity to indulge his perversion in the privacy of the dissecting room or in the mortuary without having to risk his life and reputation disembowelling prostitutes on the streets of the East End. The uterus and its appendages, the upper portion of the vagina and part of the bladder had been removed with a single stroke of the knife, which suggests a degree of surgical skill or luck, but if he had been a practising surgeon surely he would have removed the organs intact and not left part in the body.

No medical knowledge

Little can be learnt from the autopsy on Elizabeth Stride other than the fact that her throat had been cut. She appears to have been the victim of a violent domestic quarrel or a client-prostitute dispute. But if she had been murdered by the Ripper it appears she was spared further mutilations by the timely arrival of potential witnesses.

The fourth canonical victim, Catherine Eddowes, suffered severe post-mortem mutilations, the removal of part of her womb and her kidney. The latter led Dr Brown to assume that the killer had murdered her to obtain the organ and so credited him with considerable medical knowledge.

However, it seems more likely that the murderer came upon the kidney by chance and took it as a macabre souvenir only after having wallowed in her intestines as he had done with Chapman. Even Dr Brown, who had been an enthusiastic advocate of the 'mad doctor' theory, had to concede, 'Such a knowledge might be possessed by someone in the habit of cutting up animals'.

His colleague in attendance at the Eddowes post-mortem, Dr George Sequeira, agreed that it was not the work of an expert but of a man 'not altogether ignorant of the use of the knife'.

As before, the cause of death was the slitting of the victim's throat, but the most significant mutilation was the facial disfigurement. Her lower left and right eyelid had been cut through, as had the bridge of the nose, the tip being removed entirely, none of which appears to have symbolic significance nor serve an obvious purpose. If her eyes had been cut out or her ears removed, a number of things could be read into those mutilations, but odd, seemingly unrelated nicks and cuts suggest a random, teasing, tentative killer snipping here and there without a particular aim in mind. It is as if he is

Forensic photo of Catherine Eddowes

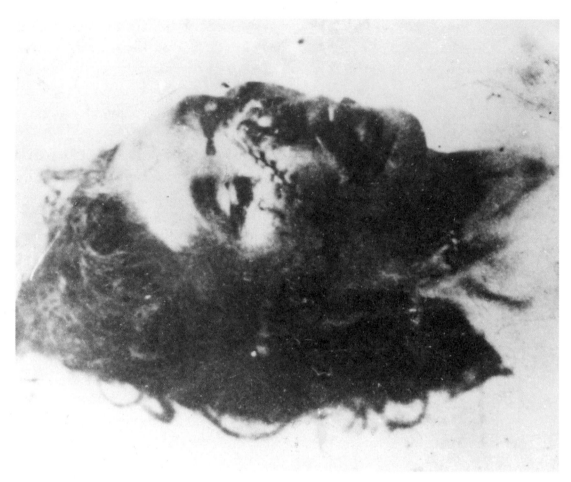

demonstrating his power over the lifeless woman like a spiteful predator tormenting its helpless prey without mercy. Her left ear lobe had been severed, but it is thought that this had been unintentional, perhaps caused by a slip of the knife when he had cut her throat.

The murder of Mary Kelly demonstrated a degree of savagery that even the hardened police surgeons found hard to view with detachment. It appears the mutilations were random and intended to render the corpse unrecognizable as that of a human being. Again, her face was disfigured, this time beyond recognition, and the heart was the only organ that was unaccounted for, though it may have been consumed in the fire burning in the grate at Miller's Court. Dr Bond thought that the object of all four murders was mutilation and that these injuries were inflicted by a person with neither scientific nor anatomical knowledge. 'In my opinion,' wrote Dr Bond, 'he does not even possess the technical knowledge of a butcher or horse slaughterer or any person accustomed to cut up dead animals.'

Eyewitness statements

So how accurate are the witness statements and which, if any, of the known suspects matches their descriptions? First of all, it needs to be remembered that no one came forward claiming to have caught the Ripper in the act, nor did any one report having seen a man fleeing the scene of the murders. In the case of Polly Nichols, there were no witnesses at all.

As far as the other slayings are concerned, the most we have are a few possible sightings of men who were seen in the company of women answering the victim's description shortly before their estimated time of death. But most of the East End prostitutes dressed alike, so few witnesses could say with certainty that it was the victims they had seen and that, of course, devalues their descriptions of the men who had been seen with them.

Besides that, the victims may have solicited several men within a very short time so that even if a witness was prepared to swear they had seen a victim in the company of a man shortly before the body was found, it does not necessarily follow that it was the same man who killed her.

Furthermore, most of the witnesses caught only a fleeting glimpse of a man whom they had no cause to take particular notice of at the time, and they did so in the half dark or by the ineffectual glow of a gaslight some yards from the suspect.

Recent research has demonstrated that eyewitnesses are notoriously unreliable even under ideal conditions and that their recollection of events deteriorates at an alarming rate. If their statements are not taken within a few hours, they are likely to confuse what they saw with people they have seen subsequently. For these reasons the descriptions given by witnesses during the Whitechapel murders are practically useless, but they are all we have.

One of the more reliable sightings was that given to the coroner at the inquest into the death of Annie Chapman by Mrs Long, who passed a man and a woman standing on the pavement outside 29 Hanbury Street just minutes before the murder took place. She had the benefit of the light of dawn, but unfortunately she did not see the man's face. He was a foreigner of dark complexion, over 40 years of age, a little taller than the deceased (approximately 165cm/5ft 5in), of shabby genteel appearance, with a brown deerstalker hat and a dark coat.

It is assumed that the term foreigner was a euphemism for a Jew, but Mrs Long may have meant to imply that he was an American or a European as she stated that she had heard him speaking as she passed, though she gave no further detail than this.

Liz Stride's murderer

An equally significant sighting was that made in Berner Street by PC William Smith on the night Liz Stride was murdered. At 12.30 in the morning, 15 minutes before Stride's body was discovered, PC Smith saw 'Long Liz' in the company of a man who the constable described as being 170cm (5ft 7in) tall, of respectable appearance, and carrying a small parcel wrapped in newspaper. He was about 28 years of age with a dark complexion and a small dark moustache, and was wearing a dark coat, dark trousers, a white collar and tie and a hard felt deerstalker hat. PC Smith was confident that it was Stride that he had seen because she was wearing a red rose which he later saw on the body of the victim.

He was about 28 years of age with a dark complexion and small dark moustache ... and a hard felt deerstalker hat

At first glance Stride's 28-year-old companion and the 40-year-old man seen with Annie Chapman appear to be two different individuals and yet both had a dark complexion, were a few inches taller than the victim and wore a deerstalker hat. As both men had been spotted in the company of the deceased just minutes before their death they merit closer inspection. Mrs Long only saw the man from the back so her estimate of his age cannot be depended upon – nor indeed her description of him as having a dark complexion. If he was instead in his mid- to late-thirties and PC Smith underestimated his age by a few years, the witnesses could have been describing the same man. The fact that he was wearing a deerstalker on both occasions suggests this is so, as it was

not a common item of headgear for inhabitants of the East End. However the terms 'respectable appearance' and 'shabby genteel' describe two distinctly different types. The former suggests a middle-class man such as a clerk, while 'shabby genteel' was a common term for a person of poor, working-class appearance whose clothes had seen better days.

Of the two, the middle-aged man is the more likely candidate for Jack the Ripper as Stride's murderer might have been her violent former lover, Michael Kidney.

Israel Schwartz, the second witness, who saw Stride being thrown to the ground, described the man as being 167cm (5ft 5in) tall, round-faced and broad-shouldered, with dark hair and a short brown moustache. He was wearing a dark jacket and trousers and a dark peaked cap. Schwartz thought he might have been about 30 years of age. His companion, the man with the pipe who followed Schwartz to the end of the street, was in his mid-thirties, 180cm (5ft 11in) with light brown hair, a dark overcoat and a black wide-brimmed hat. But Schwartz could not be certain that the two knew each other or that the shout of 'Lipski' was directed at him. It may have been intended to warn off the pipe-smoking man whom the rough might not have wanted as a witness to his assault on the woman (who we assume to have been Stride). Of course Stride may have already been lying lifeless in the yard behind the gates and the assault witnessed by Schwartz may have had nothing to do with her death. Perhaps it was the quarrel in the street which alerted the murderer and prompted him to interrupt his work rather the arrival a few minutes later of Diemschutz and his cart?

This is one case where the phrase 'there are more questions than answers' seems particularly appropriate.

Lawende's statement

A more dependable description was given by Joseph Lawende, who passed the entrance to Church Passage which led into Mitre Square minutes before the body of Catherine Eddowes was found. He testified to seeing a woman answering to Eddowes' description conversing with a man who he later described as 'rough and shabby', aged about 30, approximately 170cm (5ft 7in) tall and of medium build with a fair complexion and a fair moustache. He was wearing a grey, peaked cloth cap and a pepper and salt patterned jacket with a reddish handkerchief tied around his neck. Could this have been the same rough that Schwartz had seen 45 minutes earlier in Berner Street?

Curiously, Joseph Levy, who was walking a few paces behind Lawende, appeared reluctant to make a statement and it was later revealed that he had identified a prime suspect named by the police, a fellow Jew named Kosminski who was subsequently confined in an asylum. It is possible that Levy had recognized Kosminski that night at the entrance to Church Passage, but was unwilling to give him up to the authorities knowing that he would be hanged if found guilty. But this is pure speculation – and if Lawende had recognized a fellow Jew there is a much more likely candidate than Kosminski, of which more shortly.

Other eyewitnesses

Whatever the case, Lawende's description is perhaps the best on record, unless you accept the uncannily detailed description offered by George Hutchinson several days after the murder of Mary Kelly in Miller's Court. Hutchinson's statement must be regarded with a good deal of suspicion as it is simply too good to be true. If he had seen as much as he claimed to have done, why did he wait so long before going to the police? Had he been concocting a story in the hope of claiming a reward, or attention from the press, or did he seek to divert suspicion from himself, having learnt that he had been seen hanging around Miller's Court in the early hours of the morning Mary was murdered? Perhaps he recognized the man as Mary's ex-lover Joseph Barnett and feared being beaten if he gave Barnett up to the police, so he deliberately concocted a false and overly elaborate character?

Hutchinson described the man as 'aged about 34–35, height 5ft 6in, complexion pale, dark eyes and eye lashes, slight moustache curled up at each end and hair dark, very surly looking, dress long dark coat, collar and cuffs trimmed astrakhan and a dark jacket under lightweight coat, dark trousers, dark felt hat turned down in the middle, button boots and gaiters with white buttons, black tie with horse shoe pin, respectable appearance, walked very sharp, Jewish appearance.'

He added yet more details at a later date: 'His watch chain had a big seal with a red stone, hanging from it . . . He had no side whiskers, and his chin was clean shaven.' But would an affluent man have come down to Whitechapel to pay for sex with a 4d whore in a filthy room at Miller's Court? Also, would a man intending to butcher a woman dress so elegantly and make himself so conspicuous?

Perhaps a more reliable sighting was that made by laundress Sarah Lewis, who saw a man lurking around Miller's Court at 2.30am, half an hour after Hutchinson claimed to have seen Mary with the man of means. It was the same man who had accosted Lewis and a friend a few days earlier. He was short, aged about 40, pale-faced with a black moustache, and wore a short black coat and carried a long black bag. Such a man would conform to the description given by Mrs Long.

Earlier that evening, around 11.45pm, another prostitute living in Miller's Court, Mary Ann Cox, had observed Mary Kelly in the company of a man she described as being about 36 years old, about 167cm (5ft 6in) high, with a fresh complexion, blotches on his face, small side whiskers, and a carroty moustache. He was dressed in shabby dark clothes, dark overcoat and a black felt hat. But it needs to be remembered that both these witnesses saw Mary as much as six hours before her death.

What did the Ripper look like?

It is clear that we cannot compile a reliable description from these conflicting statements. All eight eyewitnesses disagree on almost every vital detail other than the fact that the man probably had a moustache, while several can't even agree on whether the moustache was light or dark. Three recollect seeing a man in his late thirties or early forties, while others recall a much younger man. But even if we compare the descriptions which roughly agree on age, they will disagree on other crucial details.

However, if we limit ourselves to drawing only on those witnesses who saw one of the five 'official' victims in the company of a man within 15 minutes of the estimated time of her death and set aside all testimony pertaining to the death of Mary Kelly, whose time of death is fiercely disputed, and to Elizabeth Stride, who

What did Jack the Ripper look like? It is almost impossible to compile a reliable decription from the eyewitness accounts

may not have been a Ripper victim, we can extract the following details and state with some confidence that the prime suspect was aged 28–35, 165–170cm (5ft 5in–5ft 7in) tall and had a moustache. Unfortunately that description could fit half the male population of the East End.

The best that can be said for these accounts is that they help to eliminate several suspects who are still in the running, namely Kosminski who was 24 at the time and could speak only Yiddish; Ostrog, who was 55 and uncommonly tall at 180cm (5ft 11in); Robert Donston Stephenson, who was aged 47 and had a distinctive white drooping moustache; and Francis Tumblety, who was 55 and sported an enormous handlebar moustache that no one could have overlooked. Despite the strong circumstantial evidence against Tumblety, he always seemed an unlikely suspect for the simple fact that he was a flamboyant character who would have been conspicuous in the streets of Whitechapel and who would have been unlikely to have dressed down to slum it in the East End. Of course, it goes without saying that anyone intent on murder could alter their appearance, but curiously few killers of the period did more than wear a wide-brimmed hat to cover their faces. Unless they were caught red-handed they were likely to get away with murder.

Oddly enough, the only two suspects who come close to matching the eyewitness descriptions are the long-shots George Chapman, then aged 33, 172cm (5ft 8in), with a long black moustache, sharp prominent nose and 'European' appearance, and Joseph Barnett, Mary Kelly's ex-lover, who was 30 in 1888, 170cm (5ft 7in) tall and sported the obligatory moustache.

Of course we cannot afford to dismiss the possibility that Hutchinson may have been telling the truth while the other witnesses may have been describing innocent men who happened to be in the area near the time of the murders, in which case we already have a detailed description of the Whitechapel murderer. Unfortunately, there is no way of knowing which witnesses we can rely upon. It is a frustrating fact that if the police on the scene were unable to name a prime suspect there is little chance of anyone doing so a century later.

The syphilitic butcher of Middlesex Street

There is one tool we have today which was not available to the police in 1888, and that is the practically infallible science of psychological profiling. The first rule of profiling is that a serial killer will almost always begin their criminal career close to home. Add to that the other clues offered by FBI criminal profilers elsewhere in these pages (see page 114), and the finger points at a suspect no one, to the best of my knowledge, has seriously

considered before – a mad Jewish butcher named Jacob Levy.

Under closer examination the case against Levy is a compelling one. He lived in the heart of the Ripper's killing ground with his wife and two children. He had contracted syphilis from local prostitutes, which brought on sporadic violent fits and paranoid delusions. In his disintegrating mind he would have been able to justify murdering these women and he would have been capable of committing such ferocious unprovoked attacks unburdened by remorse.

Levy also possessed the crude skill to perform the mutilations and would have

been untroubled handling, and perhaps even hoarding, human body parts as macabre trophies in his premises. Such a man could indulge his destructive tendencies vicariously on animals without arousing attention, an activity which would serve to contain his mania until such time when he would have the means and opportunity to satiate his bloodlust without fear of being caught. There were literally dozens of butchers and slaughtermen walking the streets of Whitechapel and Spitalfields in the early hours of the morning and most of them would have had blood spattered on their aprons and hands. Levy would have passed unnoticed. By all accounts he

Serial killers always begin their criminal careers near home and only widen their territory as their confidence grows

benefited from the one characteristic which helps many serial killers elude capture for so long – he looked disarmingly normal and as such would have melted into the crowd.

The right age and the right place

Levy matches both the psychological profile and the physical description, most significantly that given by Joseph Lawende, who described a man 7.5cm (3in) taller than the woman he was with. Catherine Eddowes was 152cm (5ft), Jacob Levy was 160cm (5ft 3in). He was also in the right age bracket, being 32 at the time of the murders. The reluctant witness Joseph Levy would have known Jacob Levy by sight as they lived in the same neighbourhood. It is not unreasonable to assume that Joseph's reluctance to give a statement was due to his fear of what Jacob might do by way of a reprisal.

As serial killers always begin their criminal careers near home and only widen their territory as their confidence grows, it is highly significant that Jacob Levy lived in Middlesex Street, just three streets away from George Yard where Martha Tabram was found, and 91m (100yd) from Goulston Street where a piece of Eddowes' bloodied apron was discovered on the night of the double murder. (See map, page 152) Martha is regarded by many people as the first real Ripper victim, although I am not convinced. Nevertheless, the fact

remains that all of the 'official' victims were found north of the Whitechapel Road within walking distance of Levy's home while the disputed victims lie south of that infamous thoroughfare.

When his ravings finally forced the authorities to consider Levy for committal in an asylum in August 1890, his wife admitted that 'he does not sleep at nights and wanders around aimlessly for hours'. Suspicions too must be roused by the findings of a report made by the asylum's admissions officer who concluded that Levy feared 'that if he is not restrained he will do some violence to someone; he complains about hearing strange noises; cries for no reason; feels compelled to do acts that his conscience cannot stand; and has a conscience of a feeling of exaltation.'

But perhaps the most damning clue of all is the fact that Jacob Levy died in the asylum the following year, the same year that Scotland Yard officially closed their files on the Whitechapel murders.

Summing up and verdict

It is clear from the evidence presented in the preceding pages that the real Jack the Ripper bore no relation whatsoever to the aristocratic figure in the fog portrayed in popular fiction, nor in the countless films, documentaries and dramatizations of the Whitechapel murders of 1888. As this exhaustive re-examination of the facts has revealed, the Ripper was a modern myth created

by a rabidly competitive press, every bit as ruthless as the elusive fiend himself.

Significantly, the appearance of 'Saucy Jack', the first modern serial killer, coincided with the rise of the populist press, who took advantage of the lack of hard news in the autumn of 1888 to fabricate their own. With their graphic illustrations and bold black headlines, these forerunners of today's tabloids were largely responsible for stringing together a series of apparently random and unrelated slayings and in so doing elevating an unexceptional individual to mythical status in order to satisfy the public's insatiable appetite for sensation and boost their own circulations.

Of the nine victims nominally credited to the Ripper, he probably killed only three, maybe four, the others being attributable to endemic street crime and perhaps even a copycat killer anxious for notoriety. Had it not been for an enterprising but irresponsible journalist who sent a series of hoax letters to the Central News Agency signed 'Jack the Ripper', the Whitechapel murderer would be no more than a postscript in the chronicle of crime filed away under the anonymity of his original nickname, 'the knife'. As it is, the real murderer remains anonymous to this day despite attempts by professional criminologists and amateur armchair detectives alike to put a face to the fiend who held London in fear during the 'Autumn of Terror'.

The simple fact is that no one knows the identity of Jack the Ripper, not even those who investigated the case at the time, and the chances are that we will probably never learn the truth.

It is entirely possible that Jack the Ripper as we envisage him never existed but was a composite created by the press who knew that one lone psychopath makes a better story than several insignificant individuals who happen to be operating within the same locality. A guardsman is the most likely killer of Martha Tabram, Michael Kidney probably murdered Elizabeth Stride, Joseph Barnett may have killed Mary Kelly and Jacob Levy very likely accounted for Nichols, Chapman and Eddowes.

Nevertheless the man the press tagged Jack the Ripper continues to hold a grim fascination for successive generations because he remains in the shadows and as such can be whoever we want him to be. He is the one that got away, the bogeyman of our nightmares and the central figure in the most tantalizing whodunnit in the history of crime.

Lasting impression: in Alfred Hitchcock's The Lodger *(made in 1927), a Jack the Ripper-type serial killer reappeared*

THE WHITECHAPEL MURDERS – SIGNIFICANT EVENTS

1887

26 December 'Fairy Fay' found dead near Commercial Street.

1888

25 February Annie Millwood survives stabbing with a clasp knife.

28 March Ada Wilson survives serious neck wounds after stabbing.

5 April Emma Smith dies in the London Hospital from peritonitis after attack by three men.

7 August Martha Tabram found murdered in George Yard Buildings.

31 August Polly Nichols killed in Bucks Row; Robert Anderson appointed Assistant Commissioner for Crime; Donald Swanson charged with investigating Whitechapel murders.

1 September Mrs Colwell claims to have discovered blood in Brady Street, indicating that Nichols might have been killed elsewhere.

4 September 'Leather Apron' named as suspect by press.

6 September Polly Nichols interred at Little Ilford Cemetery.

7 September John Pizer named as 'Leather Apron' by police.

8 September Annie Chapman killed in Hanbury Street; Henry James spotted outside the Forrester's Arms with a large knife; Mrs Fiddymout reports seeing a bloodstained man in the Prince Albert pub who is later identified as Jacob Isenschmid. Isenschmid is taken into custody and accused by Dr Cowan and Dr Crabb of being the Ripper.

10 September John Pizer arrested and accused of being 'Leather Apron'.

13 September Edward McKenna is arrested in connection with the Ripper murders, but is released soon after.

14 September Annie Chapman is laid to rest at Manor Park Cemetery.

17 September Isenschmid is committed to Fairfield Row Asylum, Bow, but the killings continue.

18 September Charles Ludwig is arrested after threatening two women with a knife.

19 September At the inquest into the murder of Annie Chapman, Dr Phillips raises the possibility that her uterus might have been removed for sale to a medical student who had expressed interest in obtaining specimens.

27 September Prince Albert Victor leaves for Scotland; the 'Dear Boss' letter is received at the Central News Agency, the first mention of the name 'Jack the Ripper'.

30 September Elizabeth Stride murdered at 1am in Berner Street; Catherine Eddowes murdered approximately 45 minutes later at Mitre Square. 'The Juwes' graffiti discovered at Goulston Street but erased under orders from Sir Charles Warren. Prince Albert Victor seen in the company of Queen Victoria in Abergeldie, Scotland.

1 October The Daily News publishes the 'Dear Boss' letter and the myth of 'Jack the Ripper' is created. Thomas Coram discovers a bloodstained knife in Whitechapel Road; the Lord Mayor of London offers £500 reward for the apprehension of the killer; Queen Victoria telephones the Home Office to express her shock at the murders and urge the authorities to intensify their efforts to apprehend him. The 'Saucy Jack' postcard is received at the Central News Agency and is published in that evening's edition of the Star. A deluge of hoax letters follows.

2 October Queen Victoria's psychic Robert James Lees offers to identify the perpetrator but is dismissed out of hand as a crank.

3 October Woman's dismembered remains discovered in Whitehall.

4 October Lees repeats his offer to assist Scotland Yard and is again rejected.

6 October Elizabeth Stride is buried at East London Cemetery.

8 October Catherine Eddowes interred at Little Ilford.

16 October George Lusk of the East End Vigilance Committee takes delivery of a package containing half a female kidney and the 'From Hell' letter.

7 November Francis Tumblety is arrested for gross indecency but later released.

9 November Mary Kelly is killed in Miller's Court. Sir Charles Warren resigns.

12 November Police are given a detailed description of suspect seen with Mary Kelly by witness George Hutchinson

13 November Edward Larkins informs on Antoni Pricha, who fitted description given by Hutchinson.

19 November Edward Buchan commits suicide but is not named at the time as having been a Ripper suspect. Mary Kelly is buried at Leytonstone Roman Catholic Cemetery.

20 November Annie Farmer attacked, but was it by the Ripper?

24 November Francis Tumblety escapes justice by fleeing to the USA.

30 November *Montague Druitt dismissed from his position at a school in Blackheath.*

1 December *Inspector Walter Andrews ordered to New York to investigate an unnamed suspect.*

6 December *Joseph Isaacs accused by the press of being the Ripper, arrested but charged only with theft.*

7 December *David Cohen (aka Nathan Kaminski?) arrested and subsequently confined in Colney Hatch Asylum.*

20 December *Rose Mylett killed in Clarke's Yard.*

31 December *Montague Druitt's body recovered from the Thames.*

1889

March *Whitechapel Vigilance Committee said to have been informed by police that the Whitechapel murderer had drowned in the Thames.*

24 April *William Henry Bury hanged in Dundee for murdering his wife.*

1 June *Sir Melville Macnaghten arrives at Scotland Yard in the capacity of Assistant Chief Constable. Dismembered remains of Elizabeth Jackson recovered from the Thames over several dates in mid-June.*

17 July *Alice McKenzie killed in Castle Alley.*

25 July *Another 'Dear Boss' letter delivered to Scotland Yard, signed 'Jack the Ripper'.*

10 September *Torso discovered at Pinchin Street.*

20 October *David Cohen dies in Colney Hatch Asylum.*

1891

7 February *Aaron Kosminski admitted to Colney Hatch Asylum.*

13 February *Frances Coles murdered in Swallow Gardens.*

1892

14 January *Prince Albert Victor dies; official cause of death – influenza.*

1894

23 February *Sir Melville Macnaghten writes his memorandum naming main Ripper suspects.*

1895

25 April The Chicago Sunday Times-Herald *publishes Robert James Lees' claim to have tracked and identified the Ripper.*

6 June *Pathologist Dr Thomas Bond, who was involved in the examinations of Mary Kelly, Alice McKenzie and Rose Mylett, commits suicide after suffering a long, painful illness and bouts of depression.*

1901

Robert Anderson retires and announces that the Ripper's identity was known.

1902

Norwegian Ripper suspect Fogelma dies in an American asylum.

1903

John Netley, coachman to Sir William Gull, allegedly falls under the wheels of his own carriage and is killed (date unknown).

7 April *George Chapman (aka Severin Klosowski) is hanged.*

1907

Sir Robert Anderson publishes Criminals and Crime, *in which he reasserts that the Ripper's identity was known.*

1913

23 September *Chief Inspector Littlechild writes the 'Littlechild Letter', naming Tumblety as a prime suspect.*

INDEX